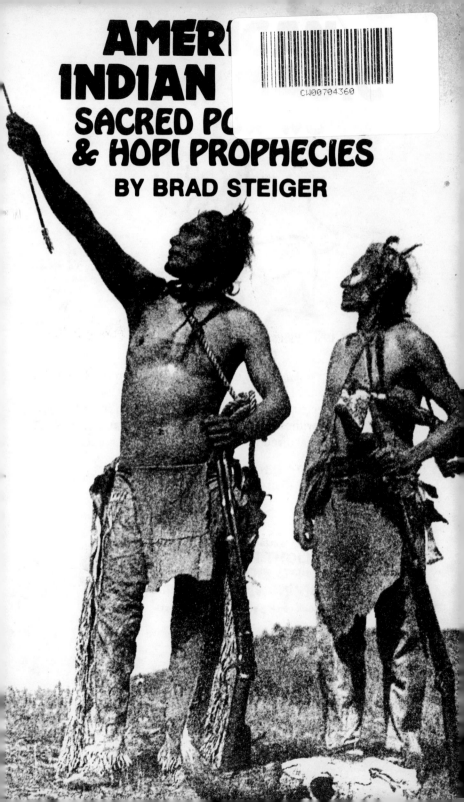

AMER INDIAN
SACRED PO
& HOPI PROPHECIES
BY BRAD STEIGER

Editorial Direction
& Layout:

Timothy Green Beckley

Copyright © 1986 by Brad Steiger

ISBN 0-938294-19-9 (Hard Cover)
ISBN 0-938294-20-2 (Soft Cover)

Published by:
INNER LIGHT PUBLICATIONS
P.O. BOX 753
NEW BRUNSWICK, N.J. 08903
Current book catalog sent free upon request.

Anthropology/New Age/Occult

CONTENTS

The author has studied American Indian magic for many years from the inside. Here, Brad Steiger is initiated into the medicine lodge of the Wolf Clan, Seneca Tribe.

CHAPTER ONE

Indian Magic Can Work For You!

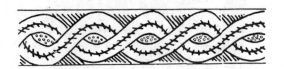

Our native American priests, the medicine men and women of the Amerindian tribes on the North American continent together with the Kahuna on the Hawaiian islands (which are now part of the United States), for centuries practiced a system of magic that was so powerful that it enabled them to control the winds and the weather, to foresee the future, and sometimes to change the future. They had the ability to heal the sick instantly, to walk over hot lava and hot coals, to read minds, to send and receive telepathic thoughts—and sometimes, it is said, even to pray their enemies to death.

* * *

After spending a great deal of time with Medicine People from many different tribes in the United States, I have put together what I believe to be the most essential elements of Medicine Power or Native American Magic. I realize it is presumptuous to try to distill into eight steps the very essence of the cosmology of the many different tribes; but it is my opinion that, in spite of great differences culturally which I found from tribe to tribe, the same basic elements of spiritual expression appear consistent. I have broken those elements down this way:

1. The vision quest with its emphasis on self-denial and the spiritual discipline which is extended to a lifelong pursuit of wisdom of body and soul.

2. A reliance upon one's personal visions and individual dreams to provide one's direction on the path of life.

3. A search for personal songs to enable one to attune oneself to the primal sounds, the cosmic vibration of the great spirit.

4. A belief in a total partnership with the world of spirits and in the ability to make a personal contact with "grandfathers" and "grandmothers" who have changed planes of existence.

5. The possession of a nonlinear time sense.

6. A receptivity toward the evidence that the essence of the Great Spirit may be found in everything.

7. A reverence and a passion for the Earth Mother, the awareness of one's place in the web of life and one's responsibility toward all plant and animal life.

8. A total commitment to one's beliefs that pervades every aspect of one's total life and enables one truly to walk in balance.

For several years now I have incorporated my own personal metaphysics with American Indian Magic. I find that it is imperative in native American magic or in any practice of metaphysics to set a time apart to enable one to enter the silence.

In one sense I do a condensed version of the vision quest. During the course of my day-to-day activities I have a daily exercise routine in which I work vigorously with barbells and dumbells, ride a bicycle and go for a long walk in order to exert my body and distract my conscious self. I find that just as one on a vision quest may deplete his physical self with monotonous and strenuous tasks in order to free the subconscious, so, for me, does the workout with weights accomplish this same goal.

After this period of exercise, I enter a hot shower (which is, in one sense, the counterpart of an instant sweat lodge). After I have towel-dried, I lie flat on my back in a quiet place, apart from everyone and all distractions, and permit whatever is to come to me from the silence easy access to my heightened state of awareness. For an added physical stimulus, I might wrap myself in a blanket, even covering my head. Such a withdrawal and sealing off increases my sensation of being totally isolated and permits me to become even less aware of my physical body and my surroundings.

One may also smoke as an aid to meditation. The American Indian smoked by way of religious observance, not for personal pleasure. I recommend a very moderate use of tobacco, but, as a physical stimulus, one can offer the pipe (I think that cigars and cigarettes would be far less preferable for such a ritual) to the four directions, upward to the Great Spirit and downward to the Earth Mother.

The puffs of smoke being carried toward the ceiling or the sky should represent one's thoughts or prayers being offered to the Great Spirit. One should use these rhythmically released clouds of smoke as focal points for concentration.

If you have achieved an attitude of calm before smoking, you should find that your thoughts and images will begin to come to you almost at once.

Traditional Medicine People carry a small bag which is filled with objects regarded as personally sacred to the bearer. If you should wish to emulate this practice, you should remember to include objects symbolic of the four elements—fire, water, air, and earth. And you should remember that these objects (and any other items that may have personal significance to you) serve as physical stimuli upon which you might meditate in order to open the channel of your subconscious.

You might wish to go out, as many native Americans do, to find your medicine stone. The medicine stone is something you can carry in your bag—or perhaps drill a hole through it and wear it about your neck on a leather thong—as a kind of physical stimulus. The great Seneca Medicine Woman, Twylah Nitsch, teaches the following guide:

If you choose a round stone, you may be quite likely a professional person, which indicates by the roundness of the stone that you are quite flexible. "Rolling stones" are often used as healing stones.

An oval stone indicates that you will learn (or have learned) the greatest amount of wisdom in the first thirty years of your life. The remaining years will be spent in searching. People who pick an oval stone are frequently very difficult to satisfy. Many lack self-discipline. By picking up an oval stone and carrying it with them, they may begin to develop self-understanding and self-responsibility.

A three-sided stone, shaped something like a pyramid, reveals an inner knowing. The people who would choose such a stone are usually good listeners and likely to follow their intuitive impressions.

The four-sided stone represents self-respect. Four is very important as a symbol to native Americans. The four-sided stone would also represent the influence of nature. The four-sided stone is one of abundance. Individuals who would be attracted to such a stone are usually very self-disciplined, not easily swayed by others, and are capable of making long-lasting friendships.

A five-sided stone represents a high level of creativity. They stand independently on each side, so someone who is attracted to a five-sided stone would be very much aware of his surroundings and be on the lookout for expressions of beauty.

The six-sided stone would be attractive to a person who has a talent for assessing the needs of others. This person would be rather selfless and would generate a great deal of trust on the part of others. In his day-to-day life he would express great sincerity.

If the stone should have, by any chance, more than six sides, it would represent an individual with great extrasensory perception..

The stone that has had a hole "drilled" in it by an act of nature is called an environment stone, and it can be worn or carried in a pouch. It is used as a reminder that we are all of the same spiritual substance.

Twylah also believes that dreams tell us something about ourselves that we do not already know. Or that they are revealing patterns, future or present, of which it would be to our advantage to be made aware.

Dream control is difficult, but it is hardly impossible to learn. Anyone can keep dream diaries and maintain a permanent record of the assistance that he is being given nightly by his unconscious—or if you will by the Great Spirit. Dream symbols are personal, and while there seem to be universal images which bear consistently similar messages to dreamers in several cultures, one must come to know himself or herself during the vision quest so that he may be able to sort out glimpses of the future from bits and pieces of psychological garbage which are being manufactured by other levels of consciousness.

Some symbols that may come to you in dreams (and their meaning in terms of the American Indian cosmology) are the following:

• *In a dream you see a toadstool—or somehow a toadstool becomes significant to you in your dream. This could be a symbol of the power of compassion. If the toadstool was standing upright, it has spiritual significance. When leaning with a broken stem, it represents a situation where compassion has been overlooked. Very often the toadstool can serve as a symbol of a reminder of a talent that needs to be revitalized or fully developed.*

• *To dream of a bee, or to see a bee in a vision or during a vision quest, is to see a symbol of an industrious, selfless, self-sufficient individual who can deal with great success and a wide range of activities.*

• *A bird sitting in a tree would represent one who has high ideals, who finds places and positions of trust and integrity.*

• *If one should dream of a rabbit that is looking toward the west with one eye shut, this indicates a disregard for the future. If the ears are upright, that represents an intense listening. If the mouth is closed, that reveals a nontalkative individual with a sense of knowing when to speak. If there is a sparkle in the eye, this suggests good health. The symbol of the rabbit means that a person is always ready to handle sudden challenges, but sometimes tends to act before evaluating the challenge.*

• *The turtle is a symbol of peace. The turtle clan is a peace-making clan within the tribal structure. Whenever the turtle is challenged, he prefers to draw within, to become silent. If you dream of a turtle, you may be dreaming of a person who is stubborn and who often is misunderstood because of his stubbornness—or who himself or herself feels misunderstood.*

• *To dream of a horse or to see a horse as your symbol during a vision quest is to see an honest worker, a faithful strong and healthy person. If the horse should happen to look tired, then you are seeing someone who should be trying to revitalize its creator capacities.*

• *To frequently dream of a cat is to dream of suspicion, and it may even be a sign of anger. A cat represents a person who is trying to be calm, but whose intensity is capable of shattering his tranquility at any time. The symbol of a cat is generally not conducive to constructive thinking.*

• *Dreams of mountains may represent lofty ideals on two levels of awareness. If there are a lot of clouds surrounding the mountains, it may indicate that certain ideals may not be on a permanent foundation.*

• *The bear, both as a symbol during visions or dreams, generally represents a family-centered individual, a devoted lover, someone who has great silent strength.*

• *To see a snake is to see a symbol of wisdom. A snake attacks only when it is provoked or challenged. To dream of a snake in connection with a particular individual would tell you that that person has the ability to develop his or her inner-knowing and inner-wisdom.*

• *To dream of a duck or a goose—or to perceive one as your totem in a vision—is to see a symbol of one who is a friend to all creatures.*

• *A dog in a dream or vision represents faithfulness, devotion—one who is always available when truly needed.*

• *A seagull represents a coming voyage. To dream of a seagull that is flying quite high is to be expressing inner-knowing and feelings of self-satisfaction.*

• *To dream of a fish that is particularly colorful, perhaps blessed with long and luxurious fins, is to dream of a person or a thing that may have too many frills to constitute a truly meaningful and worthwhile experience—or to become a trusted or worthwhile friend.*

• *To see a mouse in your dream or vision is to see a symbol of a potential to expand your awareness. The mouse also suggests that it is time to get into things that have been unused—and to make better use of possessions or ideas that have been stored away.*

7

• *A hawk represents benevolence. It represents an individual with a strong desire to be useful and to help others.*

• *The snail indicates that one is sticking steadfastly to one's routine. Depending on the size of the snail, it may represent that the routine is becoming heavy or burdensome. The snail very often represents the creative idea that will eventually come to fruition.*

• *A butterfly denotes peace and conditions that are moving at a steady pace—especially after a recent change in thinking or a rebirth experience.*

• *To dream of a water lily is to dream of a coming event of great pomp and glamour.*

• *To find a feather while on your quest is to receive advance notice of good news. We once had a feather materialize on my wife Francie's pillow when I was separated from her by a distance of 2,000 miles. Flying outside of my window at nighttime was a large black bird. I had been alerted to its presence by its pecking at the glass panes. When I called Francie to report that interesting occurrence, she found a large black feather on her pillow. The feather has strength to bring support and good will from higher intelligences.*

• *To dream of a chirping bird, actually, or to have a chirping bird land on your windowsill or beside you is to note that you will soon be the recipient of good news. There will be an event, an occurrence, or the visitation of an individual. It will bring great joy to you.*

• *To dream of a buffalo or to see a buffalo on your vision quest is to see a symbol of great force and strength.*

• *To dream of some kind of prehistoric creature, such as one of the giant reptiles, would indicate that you are about to bring forth new ideas from the old. If the symbol should appear rather violent or threatening, it probably indicates that your new ideal will not be readily accepted and that you may have to reword it to bring it into more acceptable terms.*

During the vision quest, one often acquires a personal song or sound. This personal vibration will greatly facilitate you in future meditation. If you have not received such a song or sound, don't overlook certain pieces of music which may contain nostalgic triggers that will work for you, invoking images of great strength.

Nearly everyone has a song that is loaded with particularly sentimental images. Sometimes those melodies can send you back to a particular experience. And then, after that moment has been relived, your unconscious can be soaring here and there, often returning with valuable insights.

Music has the capacity to take you into the past—then allow you to daydream or to wander mentally into areas in which your higher self can reach down and bring you up by the hand into greater awarenesses. Music is an ideal way to prime the pump, to get your creative and meditative mechanisms into full operation.

Do not neglect many fine recordings of native American music. There have been some recent New Age compositions that combine the traditional with modern recording techniques. A contemporary composer-artist whom I find particularly effective in helping me to transcend the ordinary world is Steven Halpern.

In our modern American society, one may often become rather uneasy in stating a belief in a total partnership with the world of spirits. I think you might begin by at least keeping the door open to the possibility that you may be able to establish contact with those who graduated to other planes of existence.

Under no circumstances should your contact with the spirit world be forced. A relaxed and tranquil state of mind will best permit your psyche to soar free of time and space and return with images, impressions, messages, and perhaps even an accompanying guide or a concerned entity. Each session should begin with you (when alone) or each member of your circle asking a prayer for guidance or protection.

One of the most difficult aspects that the modern man or woman has to overcome in truly practicing American Indian Medicine or any system of magic is to learn to live in a nonlinear time sense. Our society is so completely and slavishly governed by the human-made markings of linear time that we must, through meditation, stop the world and learn how to develop a magic or spiral time sense.

As I have stated repeatedly in previous books, meditation affords the most effective method I know for allowing one to break free of the boundaries of conventional time. We must always realize that central to an understanding of any system of magic is the knowledge that, for one level of the unconscious (the deepest and most spiritually attuned level), linear time does not exist. All is an Eternal Now. An altered state of consciousness properly conducted will permit you to enter that time-free, unchartered, measureless kingdom of the psyche.

At the same time, one must establish a close connection to the Earth Mother. And one must learn really to see and to appreciate all of her adornments and trappings. You must come to know that you are a part of the universe and that the universe is a part of you. You must recognize that the essence of the Great Spirit is to be found in all things—and *all* things are linked in ways that are as yet too subtle for your total comprehension. You must bear your responsibility toward all plants and animal life with dignity and not with condescension. In my opinion, a total commitment to such Medicine Power is in complete harmony with the basic belief structures of all schools of positive metaphysical teachings and should be considered complimentary to those bodies or philosophical thoughts which consider themselves to be orthodox religions.

Although I have long since abandoned anthropormorphic concepts of the Supreme Being, in moments of intense prayer I find myself speaking to the Source of All That Is (the Great Spirit) as if I truly were a child of the Father/Mother Creator Spirit. Intellectually, I know the truth of the relationship must be something very different and that to speak to *All That Is* as a Father or as a Mother is but a psychological device which is based upon my affection for my childhood images of my own parents. But the unconscious mechanism that is established enables me, I believe, to have an emotional sense of devotion and a humility which will permit me to achieve the proper psychic attunement with that Supreme Intelligence that exists beyond my conscious self.

If you have attained the proper spiritual makeup and not simply rattled off your prayers as if they were religious nursery rhymes, you can come to feel in touch with an energy source outside of yourself and you will come to feel a new power within your own being.

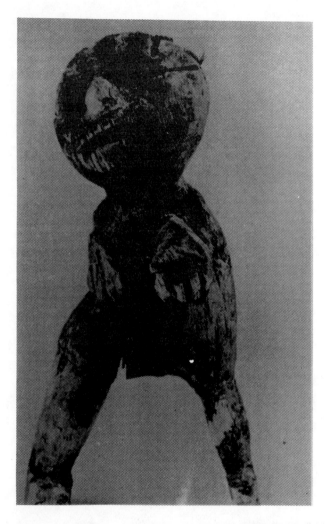

Made of wood and genuine hair, this authentic Tlingit Shaman's doll from the G. Emmon's collection is said to have incredible occult powers.

CHAPTER TWO

The Invisible Dead of Many Tribes

In the Los Angeles *Herald Examiner's* CALIFORNIA LIVING for October 13, 1968, I read an article by Wanda Sue Parrott that found a special place in my memory bank. According to Wanda, the bulk of ghost reports received by the *Herald Examiner* consisted of incidents involving the spectral manifestation of American Indians.

In one of the cases Wanda recounted, a Mrs. W. was told by the ghost of an Indian man that he would leave her apartment only if she disposed of the Amerindian artifact which she had recently acquired. Mrs. W. did so, and even though the ghost was true to his word and departed with the artifact, she found herself so unnerved by the eerie experience that she consulted a psychiatrist. The psychiatrist consoled her with the astonishing statement that there was nothing wrong with her; many of his patients had had similar experiences with the ghosts of American Indians.

"A number of San Gabriel Valley residents have shared in the Indian experience," Ms. Parrott wrote. "Men, women and children alike have reported seeing a male Indian appear in their yards, bedrooms and living rooms at all hours of the day and night.

"Most of the witnesses agree, 'He seems friendly enough. He stays for a moment or two, then fades...'"

As I interviewed Medicine People from many different tribes in the process of gathering data for this book, I recalled Wanda's article. I had long become convinced that our new age of ever-rising awareness was experiencing a return of the power and spirit of Amerindian Magic, but as I listened to an impressive number of well-documented accounts of Indian ghosts from both Amerindians and Anglos, I began to wonder what elements in addition to the rebirth of Medicine Power might be summoning these specters from other dimensions of being.

I believe that I may have found a clue to these continuing and increasing manifestations of Amerindian phantoms in the prophetic warning of Chief Seathe (Seattle) to the white men who cheated his people out of their lands with the Treaty of Point Elliott in 1855:

...Our religion is the traditions of our ancestors, the dreams of our old men, given them by the Great Spirit, and the visions of our sachems, and is written in the hearts of our people....

Every part of this country is sacred to my people. Every hillside, every valley, every plain and grove has been hallowed by some fond memory or some sad experience of my tribe....

The braves, land mothers, glad-hearted maidens, and even little children, who lived here...still love these solitudes. Their deep fastnesses at eventide grow shadowy with the presence of dusty spirits. When the last red man shall have perished from the earth and his memory among the white men shall have become a myth, these shores shall swarm with the invisible dead of my tribe....

At night when the streets of your cities and villages shall be silent, and you think them deserted, they will throng with the returning hosts that once filled and still love this beautiful land.

The white man will never be alone. Let him be just and deal kindly with my people, for the dead are not altogether powerless. Dead, did I say? There is no death, only a change of worlds.

Did the white man, imbued with the rationalization for greed which he called Manifest Destiny, convert Chief Seattle's warning into a malediction?

While the red man hallowed "every hillside, every valley, every plain and grove," the white man yearned to possess them.

While the red man believed that the Great Spirit had decreed that man must learn to live with the Earth Mother, the white man was convinced that Almighty Providence had hidden wealth and riches in the soil and in the mountains to "reward the brave spirits whose lot it is to compose the advance-guard of civilization."

While the red man knew that the Earth Mother could cradle all men to her fertile bosom, the white man's revelation told him that "...the Indians must stand aside or be overwhelmed by the ever-advancing tide of emigration. The destiny of the aborigines is written in characters not to be mistaken. The same inscrutable Arbiter that decreed the downfall of Rome has pronounced the doom of extinction upon the red men of America."

And so the white man ignored Chief Seattle's plea to be "just and deal kindly" with his people. And they laughed away his admonition that "the dead are not altogether powerless." In an era of bloody madness that has been mythologized as glorious, the west was won and the Amerindian nations were nearly decimated.

"For a mightly nation like us to be carrying on a war with a few straggling nomads...is a spectacle most humiliating, an injustice unparalleled, a national crime most revolting, that must, sooner or later, bring down upon us or our posterity the judgment of Heaven," observed a conscientious John B. Sanborn, who bore the role of a peace commissioner

16

with what dignity such an ironic title might provide. (Cheyenne (Wyoming) *Daily Leader*, March 3, 1870.)

These shores shall swarm with the invisible dead of my tribe.

"[The ghost] looks like an Indian," Mrs. [Gale] Sokol says, "and it makes more sense if it's an Indian because my house is on an old Indian burial ground..." She disappears, reappears with three Indian artifacts. "I found these Indian carvings in my backyard." [John Pascal, "Long Island Diary," Newsday, *Garden City, New York, August 4, 1972]*

At night when the streets of your cities and villages shall be silent, and you think them deserted, they will throng with the returning hosts that once filled and still love this beautiful land.

[Edward] Amberman said he did not receive a strong impression from the man with a cloak but...while on one side of Harland Street there was the impression of a group of Indians....
...The Indian, Mingo, died in 1763 and in 1898 when Mingo Street was cut in off of Canton Avenue the graves of five Indians were discovered by excavators....
...The man in the cape, [Jacklyn Berman] said, appeared to have piercing red eyes and [she] guessed that an Indian in the Colonial period would wear the type of clothing such as a cape. It was her guess that this ghost was that of the Indian, Mingo. [Richard Kent, Patriot Ledger, *Quincy, Massachusetts, August 28, 1972]*

The white man will never be alone...for the dead are not altogether powerless....There is no death, only a change of worlds.

Mrs. Potter said her husband had many encounters with the Indian before their marriage. After marriage, Mrs. Potter had her first encounter with the Indian in 1961, before a serious illness.
"He came to warn us of danger ahead," she said, "and he protected me." [Wanda Sue Parrott, CALIFORNIA LIVING, *Los Angeles* Herald Examiner, *October 13, 1968]*

Does the fact that increasing numbers of white Americans believe themselves to be haunted by Indian specters provide yet additional evidence of the power of American Indian Magic? Or are such phantoms the inevitable result of the guilt that the collective unconscious of the United States is experiencing as a more sensitive and aware nation comes to grips with the question of whether we are the posterity upon whom the Indian Wars and avaricious Manifest Destiny have brought down the judgment of Heaven?

Since Wanda Sue Parrott had written her article on Indian ghosts in California years before I began my research, I thought that I must contact her in order to learn whether she had received any additional reports of encounters with Amerindian ghosts who were "not altogether powerless."

Wanda frequently appears on radio, television, or before groups to speak on her experiences with psychic phenomena. Despite a life filled with paranormal experiences, she remains an objective and often skeptical person about planes beyond the physical. Here she describes what she learned about this phenomenon.

Once I was given an assignment to interview people in Los Angeles who claimed to have seen or encountered the "spirits" of American Indians.

One woman, who said an Indian burned her foot in bed, knew I didn't believe her story. She said, "You'll believe it after an Indian has come into your room. Then, nobody will believe you!"

I was nearly finished writing my story when I went to bed at about 11 P. M. one night in June. I fell into a very deep sleep. As I drifted off, I had been wondering how an Indian would manifest if one should come to my room. Would I be scared? Would I be able to see or hear him?

Suddenly a loud banging sound awakened me. Someone or something was knocking loudly on the center of the door. It was a full moon; I could see the door's middle shaking in the moonlight.

Then the banging stopped and the gold-colored knob started turning. First it turned one way, then the other. It was so noisy, such a rattling sound, that I knew my husband would wake up. If he could witness this phenomenon, he might not be the world's Number One psychical skeptic any longer.

I had the very strong feeling that someone was trying to reach me, desperately trying to alert me to something or get a message to me.

I was not frightened. I watched the doorknob in fascination. But when my husband did not wake up, and when the door did not open, I decided to open it myself. I did. I peered into an empty hallway, as I knew would happen.

I then went to my five-year-old son's room. He was fast asleep, as I knew he would be. He could not have been pounding on the door or trying to turn the knob.

Nothing gave ma a hotfoot, and I saw no chief with feathers, so I went back to bed. Next morning I told my husband of the experience—which lasted fully ninety seconds. Of course he said my imagination was overactive.

All that day I had the strong feeling someone was desperately trying to contact me. And when I got home and read my mail I knew I had been right. A cousin, whom I had not heard from since 1962, had seen an airmail letter. She was holed up in a motel in Iowa, suicidally depressed over her husband's leaving her. 'You are the last person in the world to turn to for help,' she wrote.

I made a long distance call immediately. Suddenly I seemed to know exactly the right words to say—and said them in about three minutes' time. My cousin did not kill herself, nor have I ever heard from her again, by letter or phone. She is apparently quite alive and busy in her new life.

And I was entering a new phase of my professional life. I was suddenly writing quite a few Indian stories and meeting many Indians from various reservations. I even spent a whole day at the Bureau of Indian Affairs, a most depressingly sterile, non-spiritual suite of technological cubicles lit with the modern day artificial sunlight, the fluorescent tube.

And I met len Fairchuk, a Salteaux Indian. Rather, Len met me. He had founded an Indian workshop where Indians in Los Angeles could create fashioned products for money, while making the transition from the reservation to the city. I did a story about Len, and met many Indians, ranging from Sioux to Pawnee.

They made me an honorary chief of the White Buffalo, crowning me with a huge beautiful paper feather headdressing made at their workshop. The White Buffalo is a symbolic spiritual group embodying the Indian spirit of all surviving tribes.

I began receiving many invitations to become an advisor to one Indian group, a counselor with another, and a volunteer worker with yet another Indian organization which was trying to help Indians establish new lives in *the city. But I had neither time nor enough energy to get involved in all these activities. My involvement remained in spirit only.*

And it seems that once a white man—or woman—is involved with the Indian spirit, it does become part of one's life on a true spiritual level.

In 1970 while trying to buy a fishing license in a drugstore in the Ozarks, I felt an intuitive urge to go browse through a comic book stand. I quit reading comics in 1948! But I went to this rack, suddenly to find myself facing a twenty-five-cent copy of Henry Wadsworth Longfellow's Hiawatha *in comic strip form.*

I opened it a few days later, after boarding a Los Angeles-bound plane at Kansas City. And I had an experience so profound I shall never forget it. I was not looking at printed pages—suddenly I was in Longfellow's land of laughing waters—smelling the crisp leaf-scented air, tasting the clear, cold waters, hearing the singing, ringing musical silence, feeling the invisible, invincible civilization that was the Indian spirit.

When my plane landed in Los Angeles, I looked around at the smog, the airplanes, the sea of cars, and sad, mad, tense people at International Airport. It was all familiar, yet strangely unfamiliar. Where were the trees, the rushing waters, the invisible air one could smell because it had a perfume of its own? I felt like an Indian transplanted into a strange city of the future, a city actively alive but spiritually dead.

And for a few moments I felt a presence near my shoulder, almost strong enough to reach out and touch. It was the presence of a naked man with only a few feathers woven into leather thongs that were draped on a few areas of his body.

I have never seen an Indian guide. But I do believe that in some way I have attuned with the Indian spirit.

In addition to her own experiences with Amerindian ghosts Wanda shared the following accounts from her personal research files with me.:

David St. Clair, author of The Psychic World of California, *was researching his book in Los Angeles in 1971. On the day he was due to interview Mae West about her true psychic experiences, he was down to his last thirty-five cents, only enough money to pay his four-mile, one-way bus fare.*

"I had been waiting for days for a check that was supposed to arrive,' the author recalls. 'But the check didn't come and it didn't come. Everybody

20

had been telling me the spirits were supposed to be guiding me, but I was wondering just how, if the spirits were guiding me, I was going to pay my motel bill."

St. Clair went to Brazil in the 1950s. A reporter, he was skeptical of spiritism and related occult phenomena. After approximately fifteen years of living in Brazil, he came back to the United States as a believer in spirits.

"But I also believe that if there are spirit guides, it's good to talk to them aloud once in a while," the good-natured Ohio-born writer says. He admits he not only talks to the spirits, but when the spirit moves him to do so, he shouts. And that is what he did the day he was down to his last few cents.

"I started cursing out the spirits. 'Goddamn you, spirits,' I said." 'This is the last time! I have had it! I didn't want to write this book. I wanted to get a nice job and settle down like other people do, but you people kept pushing me to write this book.

Now everybody says you're supposed to be guiding me. How am I supposed to pay my rent.?'"

St. Clair was combing his hair in front of the bathroom mirror as he was cursing his spirit guides. "All of a sudden this snow white feather appeared out of nowhere. It fell, right in front of me.'

"My first reaction was to look up and see if there was a pigeon stuck to my ceiling. It did shake me up.

I had been in the motel three months and hadn't seen any feathers. I took a razor blade and slit open my pillows, but they were stuffed with bits of plastic foam.

And it was ridiculous to think a feather had been stuck to the ceiling just waiting to fall for all that time.

The windows had screens. So I took it as a sign the spirits were saying, 'Calm down, David. We're still with you. We're working on it for you.' I went on the interview with Mae West. I walked home."

The next day St. Clair showed astrologist Doris Doane the white feather. She said, "That is an apport. It's probably a sign that you have an Indian guide, and he is showing you he is with you and not to be discouraged."

St. Clair later showed the feather to Jerry Quintero, who has charge of a group of metaphysical people who hold prayer groups in the Sans Jose, California area. The representative of Universal Receivers Association held the the feather and, not knowing Doris Doane had done the same, said:

21

"I get this is from an Indian, one of your guides, who is trying to tell you not to despair."

St. Clair adds: "Two days after I cursed at the spirits, my long overdue check arrived." He felt humbled. "I knew I didn't walk alone."

Over the years, I have come to respect Wanda's findings. My own research has substantiated the fact that the American Indian is a very mystical and proud people who have developed powerful psychic abilities which we could do well to learn from as the balance of this book will show.

While it may appear frightening to the unitiates, the Shaman's mask remains a very important part of the American Indian Powwow magic.

CHAPTER THREE

The Phantom
Sioux Warrior
Who Races Trains

25

The traveling salesman was making the night trip from Minneapolis, Minnesota, to Butte, Montana. He had been dozing lightly in a lower berth when he was awakened by what he later described as a "damned uneasy feeling."

"I couldn't put my finger on what was troubling me," he told a reporter for a Chicago newspaper in that summer of 1943. "There were no strange or unusual noises in the train. I could detect nothing that sounded wrong in the steady clicking of the wheels. For some reason, I decided to lift the shade of my window."

That was when he saw the apparition. Outside of his window, so close that it seemed as if he might be able to touch them if he lowered the glass, was a brightly painted Indian brave and his spirited mount. The warrior bent low over the flying black mane of his horse and looked neither to the right nor to the left. He seemed to be mouthing words of encouragement to the phantom mustang as they rapidly gained on the train.

"I've seen them five or six times after that in different parts of the Dakotas," the salesman said. "They seem to be solid flesh, but there's a kind of shimmering around them. It's like watching a strip of really old movie film being project on the prairie."

Railroad brakemen, engineers, and construction crews in the Dakotas and Wyoming have often spoken of the phantom Sioux, and his determined race with their swift and modern Iron Horses.

"They couldn't beat the trains when they were alive," said one old-timer, who knew the legend behind the spectral racers, "but they seem to have picked up some speed in the Happy Hunting Grounds."

Frederic Remington, the famous artist of the Old West, sketched the Sioux brave and his mustang from life as the inexhaustible pair raced the train on which he was riding. Remington had heard from several travelers the same tale of a determined warrior astride a big, bony mustang, who tirelessy raced the trains as the Iron Horses steamed across plains. It was as if the locomotive represented a tangible symbol of the encroaching white man, and the Sioux believed that if he could conquer the Iron Horse, his people could vanquish the pale-faced invaders. With a marrow-chilling war whoop, the warrior would come astride the train engines as they entered a wide open stretch on the prairies. The mustang would pound the plains until sweat foamed on its lean and hard body. Only the greater speed of the locomotives would at last enable them to pull away from the chanting

Sioux and his indefatigable mount. Even in life the two had seemed more phantom than flesh.

One can easily sense the great admiration Remington had for the spirit of the Sioux and his animal as his sensitive hands recreated the powerful, surging muscles of the mustang and the intensity of its master. Remington named his sketch "America on the Move."

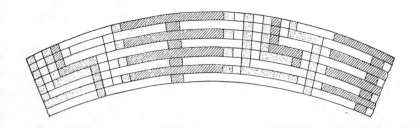

Ghost hunters, Ed and Lorraine Warren, stand at the top of a flight of stairs said to be the focal point of a series of eerie manifestations in a home located on an Indian reservation near Bangor, Maine. In the bottom photo, a glowing human form can be seen in the lower left hand window, which the Warrens maintained cannot be rationally explained.

CHAPTER FOUR

A Midnight Seance on a Indian Reservation

Ed and Lorraine Warren, a husband and wife team of ghost hunters from Monroe, Connecticut, discovered that whether or not Amerindians had spirit guides, they can certainly be the percipients of haunting phenomena. On February 15, 1972, while lecturing at the University of Maine campus in Bangor, the Warrens took time from their schedule to appear on local television and radio talk shows. In response to their broadcasted conversations about ghosts and hauntings, a Cherokee woman, who lived with her husband, a Pequot, on a reservation, telephoned the Warrens to seek their assistance in dealing with a series of manifestations in her home.

Through the courtesy of Ed and Lorraine, who provided me with a tape recording of the session, the reader will be able to experience vicariously the investigation in the midnight seance held on the reservation.

Ed Warren: *On the telephone, Mrs. S., you told me many interesting things. Could you tell us some of these now?*

Mrs S.: *A few months ago, I went out on the porch to pray during a summer rain storm. It was thundering and lightning. I saw a vision in the sky, and a strong feeling came with the vision. I saw a huge Indian, a false face, a bear, and a wolf. The bear denotes good, because he has always been food for the Indian. The bear is a sign of plenty, of survival. The wolf is a bad omen, because he is a sly and crafty creature. The false face is used in our religion, and it could have meant something about me or another person.*

The vision repeated itself two nights in a row. On the second night, about three o'clock in the morning, I saw a dark image standing in my front yard, beckoning to me. Fear came over me.

Warren: *It was beckoning to you?*

Mrs. S.: *To me. The old Indian burial ground is in our front yard and down over the bill you just came up, and it seemed to me that the image was beckoning to me and pointing toward the graveyard.*

Warren: *What did you take this sign to mean?*

Mrs. S.: *I didn't know. I got in touch with the chief of the Mohawks, and he said it could mean several different things, but he wasn't sure. Now he was gone to Hopi country, and he will ask the chiefs there, who keep up with these things.*

On the third night, this huge Indian appeared. He was kneeling and there was a fire at his knees. I couldn't see his face clearly, but the muscles in his body stood out so that I could them just perfect.

Then that ... other thing happened to me.

My husband had been at Eastport for over a week, and I was here by myself. I was sitting on the couch when this feeling hit me in the stomach. My stomach twisted, just like when you are carrying a baby—but it was on my outside. I looked down and there was nothing near me. No book. Nothing that could have put any pressure on me. A kind of silliness, a kind of trance came over me, and I went to lie down on the bed.

That same night I woke up with something pounding on the bottom of my feet. I wasn't dreaming, and I don't take any pills stronger than aspirin. I was so afraid that I couldn't move. I had heard and seen other things in the house, but they didn't bother me. This time, I was scared.

Then a ... feeling—it is hard to explain—a feeling came over me, and there was a pressure between my legs. I was afraid to move. It wasn't a dream. It wasn't a dream. It was like what you were talking about on the program.

Warren: *I was talking about a demon called an incubus that can sexually attack a woman, or a succubus that can attack a man.*

Mrs. S.: *Well, this really happened. I haven't told my husband completely. I have been afraid to tell people all of what happened. But the memory of the feeling that came over me has nearly faded.*

Lorraine Warren: *You are lucky that you can erase it from your mind.*

Mrs. S.: *The grave incident is fading, too. But the footsteps keep sounding, and they are not the result of the house settling. My husband has even nailed the door shut to the one room, but we still find the door standing open.*

This is why I asked you to come here; I want you to tell me if there is something evil in this house. If it is not evil, I want it to stay, because I think the spirit of the huge Indian is trying to tell us something. The tribes are coming together. The Indians really do have powers, but they don't always know the meaning of what they do. I am afraid that because you are white people the Indian spirits here may resent you.

Lorraine Warren: *There is resentment here.*

Warren: *Lorraine, you told me when you first came in here that you felt as if you would be forced to your knees. Why did you say that?*

Lorraine Warren: *When I came in the door, I felt depressed. I didn't even want to sit down. I felt as if I wanted to drop to my knees.* (To Mrs. S.) *Can I get to that bedroom through here?*

Mrs. S.: *No.*

Lorraine Warren: *Could you ever?*

Mrs. S.: *Yes, at one time that was a dining room and this was a serving door in through here, but it is all closed off now.*

I forgot to tell you that after my vision in the thunderstorm, a ball of red light appeared. I was depressed that night, too, and I had been praying. I do not go to Catholic church any more. I do my praying and my tobacco burning by myself.

Warren: *How old is the young man who has experienced different things in the house?*

Mrs. S.: *He will be twenty in August. He is bothered by these things, and he will tell you about them.*

Warren: *Do you think that he might have brought something into the house here when he came to live with you?*

Mrs. S.: *No, this place has been this way for a long time. There are people on the island who won't even come into my house.*

This house was really a mansion at one time. The governor even lived here. No one knows how long this house has been here. There is no record. The old people don't remember.

One time a white man who is married to an Indian came here and told me that he would sleep upstairs. He has been to some of the religious ceremonies and he understands a good deal of them. He lay down, but he soon came down. He said he heard things, and he knew that he wasn't wanted.

Lorraine Warren: *There is someone here now who resents our being here. The reason I say that is because here on this part of my hand there is a lot of pressure, a lot of pressure, and that feeling of wanting to go down on my knees! It is as if something wants to force me down.*

(At this point, W.M., the young Indian who had boarded with the S. family before his marriage, arrived to answer question for the Warrens.)

W.M.: *I was just about brought up in this house. My great-great-uncle used to own this house about fifty years ago. This house is one the oldest on the island. It is over two hundred years old. This used to be one of the most beautiful homes on the island until a certain family moved in here, and they just wrecked it. When the S.s moved in, they fixed it up surprisingly well for the condition it was in when they came.*

Warren: *What were some of the things that happened to you in this house?*

35

W.M.: *I used to stay in the front room, and I used to lie in bed and watch the stairway door open. Mrs. S. had a huge box filled with baskets that was really heavy to move, and there was a rack of clothes there. I used to watch that door open and the box and everything move.*

These things didn't really bother me, because I have had such experiences ever since I was a kid. (W.M. told the Warrens that he is able to predict death on the island with a regular and a high degree of accuracy.)

Warren: *That is interesting, because since you have a certain degree of clairvoyance, you might be able to get things in this house that others would not.*

W.M.: *One day I was sitting here reading the paper, and I was talking to my girlfriend—now my wife—on the telephone. The television wasn't on, but I was watching the screen. All of a sudden, the dogs started barking, and they came running out here. I could see the doorway reflected in the screen, and I could see the figure of a man standing there.*

Warren: *Was the figure white ... black ...?*

W.M.: *It was a dark figure, I was more intrigued than frightened, but the figure stood there for several seconds.*

Mrs. S.: *Several times you were awakened by a punch on the shoulder. You would wake up, find no one in the room, then come out and ask me if anybody had been in your room.*

W.M.: *Yeah. Every time the stairway door opened, things would go on for five or six minutes. Sometimes the clothes on the rack would spread apart, and I could feel a cold breeze go right my me. It was that strong. I wondered sometimes if it would blow the curtains down as it went by.*

Mrs. S.: *The same thing has happened to me in this corner, and it is completely blocked off. But several times I have felt the cold touch either my legs or my arms in that corner.*

Now it was midnight, and Lorraine, who is a light trance medium, indicated that her sensitivity told her it was time to hold a seance.

Ed recalls that it was a very cold, windy, bleak night, just the kind of evening that people would visualize as being ideal for a seance. Although their visit to the S. home was to have been a secret, more than twenty curious Indians had arrived to kibitz the white medicine people. Ed pleaded too many people for an effective seance and managed to thin the ranks. A skeptical reporter and a photographer doggedly insisted upon staying to observe the proceedings.

"I was uncomfortable because of the persistent sensation that something wanted to force me to the floor," Lorraine said, "but I went into a light trance in spite of this psychic harrassment.

"I got the name Priscilla, and she made herself so very clear to me," Lorraine told me. "Again, I felt as if I were actually being forced to the floor. I felt as though she were married to a man who was a very dominating person, a very cruel person.

"I saw a cemetery. A small white building with little diamond-shaped latticework. A short white fence around a number of graves. I knew that Priscilla had been buried inside that fenced-in area," Lorraine said.

"Priscilla was so clear to me. Then I saw her husband, a tall, blond man, who stood on a rock with his arms folded."

Ed Warren said, "Now, of course, Lorraine had no way of knowing names, Brad, but the Indians told me that a young Indian girl named Priscilla had married a white man, who had treated her in a cruel manner. They had lived in this home, and he used to stand on a big rock out back with his arms folded. I was surprised that Lorraine would pick a white man living on a Indian reservation, but I was told that he had filled some official capacity. When I said that I had not seen the big rock in back of the house, the Indians said that it had been blasted away long ago.

"He is buried just a couple of blocks away in a small cemetery. Priscilla, according to Mrs. S., is buried in a fenced-in area. There is also a small white building with diamond-shaped latticework near her grave.

"The sensation Lorraine experienced of being pushed down is one of the great negativity, often found in cases where demonology is concerned. The older Indians testified that the husband had been very cruel to his young Indian wife. Perhaps this domineering personality lives on in this old mansion. Right after the seance, the photographer shot what appears to be a whitish figure in the window."

If one wishes to accept the spiritistic hypothesis, it would appear that the same personality who sought to abuse and to possess completely his Indian wife, may now be seeking to torment the Indian woman who occupies his home. Mrs. S.'s vision of the bear, the wolf, the mask, and the huge, muscular Indian man may be interpreted as either evidence of the protective element within her medicine summoning her own guide from the spirit world, or as an example of the symbology of the Amerindian unconscious seeking to inform Mrs. S. of some external or internal threat to her psychic or physical well-being. There is no way of knowing how much

37

Mrs. S. knew of the story of Priscilla and her abusive white husband and whether or not domestic turmoil may have caused Mrs. S. to identify with a tortured wife. Neither is there any clue whether the alleged incubus attack may have been an example of sexual psychopathology or actual demonic invasion.

With the information available, we can but conclude with the Warrens that some psychic presence maintains a hold on that eerie mansion on a Maine Indian reservation.

In the motion picture Poltergeist, the terrifying haunting took place over an Indian burial ground. Such occurrances are common. This site near Williamantic, Connecticut, has its share of ghosts, mysterious fires and other inexplainable phenomena. Visitors report being nausea, and there is a powerful "vibration" said to emanate from this mass Indian burial ground (Photo credit: Gordon Alexander).

CHAPTER FIVE

A Haunted House on
Sacred Burial Grounds

Gordon Alexander, a photographer from Mystic, Connecticut, told me of a woman whose family had constructed a new home in the immediate proximity of an Indian burial ground.

According to Gordon, Louise Abel (not her real name), her husband, and children had learned just how thin the line can be between the living and the dead, especially if one chooses to build his house on sacred ground. The Abels wish no publicity, and Louise consented to an interview on my promise that her real name and the name of their village would be kept secret.

Louise Abel: Down and back behind my house and in our area, a great many Indians were slaughtered, and their land was taken away from them. There is a mass burial site where many of these poor, tricked Indians were piled in and covered up.

"What kind of manifestations have you observed, Louise?"

Mrs. Abel: All sorts. Every kind of visitation and poltergeistic manifestations. Even the nonbelievers can see the images projecting themselves.

"Has there been any communication at all?"

Mrs. Abel: Yes, but the problem is that we have been getting a lot of Indian words, and we have no idea how to interpret them.

"Have there been any communications in English?"

Mrs. Abel: Yes, there have been some who have come through and tried to give us the English translations. Since the manifestations, I have begun to work quietly with some groups interested in psychic matters, and we have just been waiting for someone to come along who might break through and be able to understand what is happening.

"And your home is not some three-hundred-year-old New England mansion?"

Mrs. Abel: Ours is a new house, only three years old; but we built it near the burial ground. You know, it is impossible for the kids to play drums or certain music without bringing on manifestations. That song "Cherokee Nation" used to bring about a really strange reaction. Before I realized what was happening, the kids would play it, and then everybody would kind of slump over and begin to walk differently. I had to stop them from playing it because it was just getting too powerful. It was drawing too much from us.

43

"Did anyone in the area ever report such manifestations before you built your home there?"

Mrs. Abel: It seems these things have been happening for years. Perhaps some kind of psychic vortex was created here because of the way the Indians were tricked out of their land and the way their lives were cut short. I feel the whole area here has been saturated with negative vibrations. In our case, our home often receives violent slams during the night, and we can often hear drums beating. Other people here have also heard them.

Once we were drawn to a particular spot on the lawn, and when we looked back at the house, we saw projections all over. They were the most fantastic and beautiful things I have ever seen in my life. We saw Indians, early settlers. It was one of the most fascinating experiences I think I have ever been through in my life.

"Did that occur at night or in daylight?"

Mrs. Abel: That happened in broad daylight. Now, of course, when the moon is full—especially in August, September and October—you are more apt to hear the drums, although we are certainly not devoid of them at other times. On some nights, you can see what looks like masses of Indians carrying torches. They seem to be gathering for some kind of ceremony.

"Since you seem to have some degree of psychic sensitivity, do you think that these spirits may be gathering in your home in an effort to use you as a channel to get some particular message out to the people of today?"

Mrs. Abel: I do feel that this may be the case. Those of us in our psychic study group feel that they are desperately asking for help so that they might stop some of the ecological destruction that is taking place in the area.

One word that we have received quite often—and I am attempting to trace its meaning—sounds something like *Naw-has-ee.* I don't know if that is a name, a greeting, some kind of plea for help, or what it could be. It is difficult to understand these things unless you have someone helping you from a higher spiritual vibration.

If the Amerindian Medicine People whom I have interviewed are correct in their interpretation of the signs which have begun to proliferate in the last decade, then we are at this time receiving a great deal of help from a higher spiritual plane.

Not everyone may be sensitive enough to perceive spectral members of vanished Amerindian tribes, but all men and women who want to learn to achieve harmony in their lives may gain spiritual strength from the Resurrection of the Great Spirit. If the manifestation of Indian ghosts that throng our cities and villages in the silence of night offers dramatic evidence that the line of demarcation between worlds of being is growing ever thinner and less strictly defined, then one has but to attune himself to Amerindian prophets and teachers to learn that the power, richness, and relevance of Amerindian magic is being restored. The teachings tell us that the Great Spirit will once again be recognized as the primal mystery that permeates every hillside, every valley, every plain and grove, every part of this country. If we permit a commitment to the Great Spirit to fashion our dreams and our visions, then not only will we change our lives, but our world, and despair and defeat will give way to joy and freedom.

Since the birth of Spiritualism in America, it has been common for Indian spirit guides to materialize during a seance. It is said that the reason for this is that the departed Indians, having been close to nature, have less trouble crossing the veil from one dimension to another.

CHAPTER SIX

The Spirit World is Always Near

We have already noted that the belief that the barrier between the world of spirit and the world of man is a very thin one is an integral part of Amerindian Medicine Power, but we have yet to examine the phenomenon of the "shaking tent," wherein the medicine man displays his mediumistic gift. The shaking tent ritual seems quite likely to have originated among the Eastern tribes, such as the Huron, the Algonquin, the Chippewa, and several of the Canadian tribes.

The medicine man constructs a lodge or tent in which he is to sit—sometimes naked or bound tightly with rawhide—during the ritual (one thinks of the Spiritualist minister's spirit cabinet). He lights his pipe, offers its smoke to the four directions. When the invocation has been made, the people sit in silence and watch to see the spirits come. The medicine man sings and a few chanters join. The lodge begins to shake. There is a noise and confusion thought to be the sound of spirits arriving from the four corners of the earth. The first spirit to arrive is that of an earth spirit, whose function will be to interpret for the others. Whenever a spirit arrives, a heavy blow is heard on the ground and the lodge shakes violently. When all of the spirits have arrived, the ethereal council begins. The sound of many voices is heard in the lodge, each voice distinctly different from the others. The people sit listening to the sounds in silent awe and expectation. The sacred lodge is filled with spirits of great power that have come at the bidding of the medicine man. The messages may now be given.

Those assembled may expect to receive information which will reveal the cause of certain maladies and will dictate the course of future actions. Someone wishes to know what illness besets her child. Another asks where they will find the body of an uncle who drowned in the lake. A grandmother soberly inquires if her man's spirit has been permitted to enter the Place of Departed Spirits. After each question—if the presents of tobacco are deemed acceptable—the lodge is roughly shaken and a spirit gives a direct answer.

Such tents and lodges are still used by both Amerindian medicine people and Spiritualist mediums. In the August 1969 issue of *Fate* magazine, W. D. Chesney—who describes himself as an ardent, life-long Spiritualist—tells readers how to build "A Trick-Proof Spirit Cabinet":

It consists of a cone-shaped tent made of opaque material with only one opening to permit entrance. Its heavy cloth floor is glued and sewed to the tent. The very peak of the cone is left open—but securely screened—for ventilation and other ventilation holes around the base of the teepee are also screened. Peepholes with hinged covers are provided, should investigators wish to look within the teepee....Once constructed, the teepee is completely portable and can be taken anywhere and set up in a few minutes. It may be suspended from a tree branch or from a simple tripod made from three poles tied at the top.

Chesney, in addition to giving precise directions for the spirit teepee's construction, relates some eerie anecdotes involving its usage.

"I have witnessed genuine materializations of discarnate spirit entities," he writes. "I lived among the Indians in [Oklahoma] for many years and I saw Caucasian mediums with Indian guides [spirit controls] produce almost unbelievable phenomena."

Chesney believes, as do many Spiritualists, that American Indian spirit guides provide the strongest links between the worlds of spirit and flesh.

On the wall opposite my writing desk I have a magnificent chalk drawing of my Amerindian spirit guide, Big Arrow, which was presented to me by the Spiritualist artist Stanley Matrunick. Years ago, I made a present of an antique Amerindian bust from my study to a medium friend, who had told me that it was the exact image of her guide, Shooting Star. In essence, since the advent of modern Spiritualism in 1848, we have had a native Anglo-American religion based upon metaphysical insights of the Indian in which the alleged spirits of Amerindians serve as intermediary "saints," who channel information through mediums, guide the confused spirits of the recently deceased to higher planes of spiritual development, and make these same spirits available for communication with their loved ones.

Recently, I asked the well-known Chicago medium and former Spiritualist minister Deon Frey why Indian spirit guides were so popular with Spiritualists:

The American Indian was close to Nature and already in the proper vibratory force when the Europeans arrived on this continent. The whole secret to metaphysics is getting in tune with the Universe. When you are in tune with the Universe, your awareness opens naturally. You become a part of all. Because the Indian was close to Nature and was in this vibratory force, the Indian spirits have a great strength and power. They come through [to the medium] much easier than other spirits do. Their great strength makes you know that they are really living and that they are really a part of this great creative force which is in existence.

In about 1948, when I had a Spiritualist church, I used to hold seances in the basement. I used to sit on the cabinet [[n the manner of the medicine man in his "shaking lodge"] for materializations at least three times a week. Because of my meditations and my regular sessions, great strength was building up. One night the power was so strong in my cabinet that I left it and walked out among the people in the circle.

No sooner had I taken a seat when an Indian [spirit] walked out of the cabinet and crossed the room to stand in front of me. He was all dressed in his feathers and everything. He stood right on my toes to let me know that he had weight and substance. When he turned to walk back to the cabinet, why, it almost pulled my solar plexus out! He was using my energy to help him materialize.

This Indian spirit materialized in front of all those people to show that such things are possible. Indian spirits especially are able to get the right vibratory force built up at the right time so that they may appear. They may not stay too long, but at least they make you aware that they are really there.

One of the greatest lessons that the white man has to learn is that even though he did terrible things to the Indian, the Indian spirits love him and would like to try to help the white man. They claim that one day they will be leading the white man, because this is their mission. They are a forgiving race and have great spirituality.

Mrs. Vada Hill provided me with a report of a sitting with the well-known medium Charles Swann at Camp Chesterfield, Indiana, on July 30, 1972, during which his spirit guide, Crazy Horse, materialized.

Mr. Swann's basement is paneled, and this same paneling has been placed around a support which is several feet out from the four walls. Crazy Horse told us he wanted to show us his coup stick. He said he would pass it in front of us so we could see it. From my position, the stick moved horizontally from the darkness on the left toward the right, then left into the darkness again. About two and one half feet of the stick was visible at one time. Each feather represented a brave deed. As the stick was being passed in front of us horizontally, the feathers hung straight down.

Then Crazy Horse told us that he was going to materialize to show us that he was a handsome Indian. He appeared, life-sized, in bust form. Instead of a perfect profile, his head was turned toward us, perhaps an inch.

All these materializations were taking place, not in the very center of the room, but well away from any wall, the bottom edge of the "pictures" being approximately four and one half feet from the floor. These displays were very much like "old-time" movies, the film of which had dulled with age from black and white to a brown and white. I am saying this to explain the color, not the outline of the pictures. They were complete in themselves, and were not "run" on something used as a screen or backdrop.

Al G. Manning, a Spiritualist minister who conducts the unique ESP Lab in Edgewood, Texas, told me that when he began seeking spirit contact in the late 1940s and early '50s, the first spirits he encountered were those of two American Indians:

It began with meditation in front of a mirror. They would project their symbols on my forehead. It was kind of frightening at first. Imagine seeing a full owl's head with all the intricate feathers appearing on the bare part of your forehead and going on up into your hair, for instance. This Indian gave me the name Wise Owl, and he became a very good friend and guide on the intellectual level.

When the other came to me, I would see one eye appear in my hairline and the other on my forehead. Then I would see the long, slender, and very hairy face of a fox. This spirit gave me the name of Cunning Fox. The two of them worked with me for several years before I had much in the way of other spirit contact.

The spirit of a medicine man named Wild Eagle comes often to assist us with our healing work. When he manifests, one can smell a peculiar kind of herbal incense. One night there were about twenty people in the room, and I looked up to see the bright spirit form of Wild Eagle in the corner. He was wearing the traditional buffalo horns of the medicine man, and everybody in that room will guarantee that they knew a spirit was there.

When we do our healing work, we ask a little mental prayer requesting the spirit people who are near to assist us in bringing the right energies to us. We work on the chakras, or psychic centers, to clean them out; and we also apply the light energy directly if there is a bad problem on the leg or the arm or somewhere.

When the medicine men participate in the healing work, things usually become a bit more dramatic. It is my experience that when they assist us, there is a good flow of energy. You feel the chakras cleaned out and you have put the trouble aside in a period of two or three days—or two or three weeks, depending on how bad the situation was.

Bess Krigel is an English teacher in the Chicago public schools, an instructor in ESP at Maine Township Adult Evening School in Des Plaines, and minister of the Church of the Divine Spirit of the Living God, 3300 West Lawrence Avenue, Chicago:

As you may know, Indians thought that they went to the "Happy Hunting Ground" after dying, and that their duty was to come back and help their fellowman. As a result of this belief, the Indian went to an astral plane close to earth, where his spirit could touch the earth plane easily. Spiritualists find it very easy, then, to use Indians as helpers and assistants on this plane.

I have a wise old medicine man, Red Arrow, who is one of the guides and helpers at my church. He is a stately old wise man, full of dignity and knowledge, a keeper of wisdom and a disseminator of universal truth.

Recently, a woman of about forty come into my church. She was very tall and erect, wore moccasin-type shoes, and styled her long straight black hair into two plaits. She had high cheekbones and a dark, olive complexion. When I got into her vibrations I received a strong Indian influence, and I "got" her working with her hands making baskets and making pictures with seeds and berries.

She laughed and told me that she had nothing to do with Indians, but she did admit that she liked to work with her hands on the projects I had mentioned. She added that she was of German descent.

German! With that peculiarly erect carriage, long black hair, and dark skin?

"I love Nature and love to do handiwork projects connected with it, but I know no Indians. I have always worn my hair like this, too. long before long hair was fashionable. My husband likes it this way, too."

She was the walking embodiment of an Indian maiden. This is a direct past-life influence making itself known in the subject's dress, appearance, and hobbies.

Whether one cares to explain the phenomenon by citing a collective guilt response or an idealization of a people who live a less complicated life next to Nature, the fact remains that here in the United States alone we have more than 250,000 members of Spiritualist churches who have built a cosmology around the Amerindian. Spirits of departed Amerindians are called upon for healing, for material and spiritual guidance, and for personal support in any number of earth-plane undertakings. Just as the Roman Catholic has his saints to serve as intercessors and intermediaries, so has the Spiritualist his Indian guides. Icons of Indian guides are found in nearly every Spiritualist home and are available for sale at every Spiritualist camp, convention, and meeting place. Indian medallions are worn about the neck in the fashion of rosaries, and Amerindian icons even take the place of dashboard saints in Spiritualist automobiles.

"Indians can be used to find parking places," Bess Krigel told me. "My friend Robert Quinliven told me about this several years ago. Now when I need them to clear my way through traffic jams or to find parking places, I call out (to myself of course!), 'Indians, clear the way through this jam.' Or, 'Indians, get me a parking place near this place.'

"Another medium, Fred Haase, told of one time when he circled the block three times looking for a parking place after he had sent his Indian out. Fred got very irritated at the failure of his Indian to find the place and said, 'Chief Thunder Cloud, you've certainly fallen down on the job.' With that, a car suddenly pulled out right in front of Fred, barely missing his car. Fred said he very sheepishly apologized to his Indian after parking his car."

Amerindian spirit guides are summoned for instruction in better living here on the earth plane, as well as being relied upon for guidance to Summer Land, the Spiritualist equivalent of the "Happy Hunting Ground." Most of the guides' sermons, however, give evidence of ecumenism and liberally incorporate elements of Christian and Eastern philosophy. Great Bear, a spirit teacher, had these words on "The True Reality of Freedom" recorded in *The Golden Era*, a publication of The University of Life:

...There shall not be embarrassment that one shall express of love. There shall not be the barriers—the bars that shall be set in the way that there may be the expression, one for another. For it was said in the words of the man Jesus, Honor thy God and love thy God, with all thy heart and soul, and love thy neighbor as thyself. Without definition, my children,

without boundary, without decree; it was not said love only a little bit. It was not said love only that which may be displayed within the jaded eyes of society. Rather was it said, Love thy neighbor as thyself.

While traveling near Albuquerque on January 30, 1962, Yolanda, who channels "interdimensional communications" for Mark-Age MetaCenter, Inc. of Ft Lauderdale, Florida, received a communication from a higher plane that told of her previous incarnation as Princess Lobo-Tan of the Tanoan tribe.

According to her vision, the young Indian maid had been trained in the mystic arts and had been accepted as the prophesied woman-child who would lead the Tanoans back to the Great Spirit. However, when she demonstrated friendliness to the Christian missionaries, the princess was declared a traitor and made an outcast. The Spaniards called her Lobo-Tan—Lobo for wolf, Tan for the Tanoan tribe. Left to wander, Lobo-Tan was captured and tortured by a band of marauders, who eventually took her to the Grand Canyon and threw her into the chasm to test her powers. Although they searched for her corpse, they never found it. Thus Lobo-Tan came and left the earth plane under mysterious circumstances.

On January 31, Yolanda was directed in a meditation to go to the Sandia Mountains...at the eastern edge of Albuquerque. She was told that spiritual initiations have taken place in these ranges for centuries, and that the Indian astral forces...were they to be united, would meet them there. This would result in Yolanda receiving the powers she had as Lobo-Tan, so she would be able to charge the mountain with divine power and love, thus aiding the devic forces to eliminate the dangers inherent in the area resulting from atomic experimentations.... From *Linking of Lights*, Vol. 6, *New Paths with AmerIndians* (Miami, Fla., Mark-Age MetaCenter).

At the foot of the Sandia Mountains, Yolanda made contact with Black Cloud, an Indian spirit guide, and performed an "inner plane ceremony" that brought forward many messages, among them the following prayer-statement:

We are all brothers. As brothers, we must come together under the Great Father Spirit which created us all. With this pledge, all powers of accumulation will be given for these deeds. All forgivenesses are sealed in the heart of each man and each leader, who is responsible to his many lives and to his many pasts. With this understanding, we carve new paths into the future, that all men can walk the one path and discover the one goodness and become the one heart.

Love is the key. We understand this and we shall live this. All is in readiness. Many moons will pass across the Earth's sphere before we know all the good that shall come to pass because of this time together and dedication. We kneel to the Spirit in each thing that exists. In this way we recognize the Great Spirit which is in all things.

So let us love one another and hunt for the future that the Great Father has created, and for which we still hunger. Our thirst is for righteousness and truth. We call upon the rain clouds to show us we are true sons of the Great Spirit and to nourish our bodies and our minds and our souls and to cleanse us as well as to feed us.

We understand the depths of these things and the symbols which we perform, because we are true Indians. An Indian is a son of the Great Spirit which exists and is not seen. This is the meaning of the Indian brotherhood. All men, then, are Indians as we are, from our birth and unto the end of time.

We acknowledge all that has taken place and we accept it peacefully; peacefully and for the good of all things, that they may become true brothers and Indians, in the sense of the Father who created us to care for the land, to protect the land, and to pass the land on to the next generation who follows our footsteps. Amen. I speak in the name of all brothers in all lands, because the land of all is one land.

On Thanksgiving Day, November 23, 1972, the spirit teacher Black Cloud contacted Nada-Yolanda with these thoughts:

Let us collapse time and capsule all events, making this day as though it were the first true Thanksgiving Day. Our Indian astral forces are in agreement and united that we should begin anew in '72. Starting from now, we will work in true spiritual harmony and brotherhood, as we intended and tried to do on that first feast day more than three hundred years ago.

Let us erase the karma that exists, burying our grievances, our mistakes and our misunderstandings of one another through love and cooperation. Let us go forward from this day onward giving thanks to our Great Spirit, sharing together the harvest of all our labors as true sisters and brothers of the One, our Father-Mother God.

The items on his necklace have always been of special significance to the medicine man, as were the garments he wore. The jacket below was once worn by the great warrior mystic, Sitting Bull, and is still said to bestow great magical powers on anyone who possesses it. (Top photo credit: Field Museum; bottom: Darryl Henning, Luther College Anthropology Dept.)

CHAPTER SEVEN

The Indian Curse That Destroyed A State Capitol

The lovely young girl finally stopped laughing at the man long enough to reply to his question. "Marry you?" she echoed his words with the sting of feminine mockery. "Do you really think that I would come live with you in some wigwam in the woods? I'm no squaw!"

The stoic features of the Algonquin chieftain sank into a mask of sorrow. He had been attracted to the beautiful French girl from the very first time that he had ventured into Kaskaskia, the first capitol of Illinois. Now, his offer of marriage had been spurned.

"I will offer your father many ponies in addition to the furs that I have brought today," the Algonquin said hopefully, ignorant of the ways of the white man's frontier which allowed a girl to choose her own husband. Perhaps in the Old Country the girl's father might have been tempted by such an offer to "buy" his daugher. But here, in the New World, a father no longer arranged his daughter's marriage.

"Take your smelly old furs away and stop bothering me!" At her angry shout, the girl's husky brother and a number of villagers began to move menacingly toward the rejected Indian suitor. They needed little excuse as it was to tack an Algonquin's hide to a barn door. The fledgling government had ordered that they attempt to live in peace with the Indians, but surely no government official would condone an Algonquin trying to molest a white woman.

The chieftain, infuriated by the rejection of his proposal, leaped onto his pony and glared at the villagers. He knew that there was not enough time to reclaim his furs, but he would have plenty of time to pronounce a malediction on the village of Kaskaskia.

With an angry shout, he cursed: "May the filthy spot on which your church stands be destroyed, may your homes and farms be ruined, may your dead be torn from their graves, and may your land be a feeding place for fishes!"

A rock struck the Algonquin on the forehead and he swayed dizzily on his mount. He touched his fingers gingerly to the wound and frowned at the blood on his hand. He leaned forward on his pony and spat on the ground; then he raced out of the village.

Because the Algonquin pronounced his curse in 1819, it is unlikely that he lived to see it fulfilled. But, in 1881, the flooding Mississippi River acted as the agent that carried out the Indian's curse, item for item. The violence of the waters completely destroyed the Church of the Immaculate Conception. The flood drowned the crops of the French settlers and scooped out the dead from their graves. Nearly all of the houses in the village were carried away by the rampaging waters.

As the ultimate fulfillment of the curse, the turbulent waters created a new channel, placing the original village of Kaskaskia in the middle of the stream—a true "feeding place for fishes."

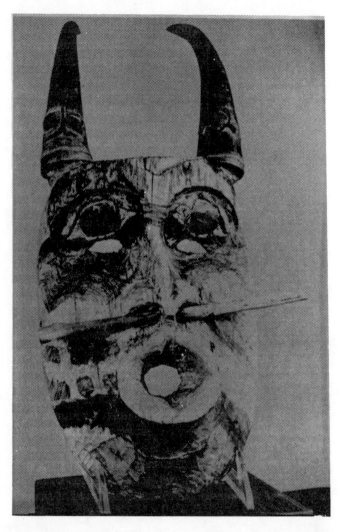

Evil spirits known as Chindi are often called upon to render deadly curses. This mask made of wood, goat's horn, and quill was probably an attempt by a medicine man to depict such an entity. (Photo credit: John Tiffany)

CHAPTER EIGHT

The Terrible Power Of The Chindi

It began in 1825, when a man of the Navajo Long Salt family became ill because of nightmares caused by the restless spirit of a slain enemy. The man's brothers sought assistance from an old, blind medicine man from the Tsegi country, and, at their request, he held a three-day *b'jene* (sing) over the tormented sleeper.

For part of his pay, the medicine man asked five butchered sheep from the Long Salts' valuable flock. But since the flock was grazing at some distance from the village (and the old man was blind anyway), the Long Salts assigned to the task of slaughtering the animals decided to substitute five wild antelope in their place.

The old medicine man was escorted home with the honors due his position and awarded the five carcasses. With the heads and the lower legs removed at the knees, even the Long Salts who made the presentation had been unable to detect the substitution that certain lazy and deceitful members of their family had perpetrated.

A few weeks later, an older member of the Long Salt family died. Although some deemed it strange that the old man had not suffered any illness before his death, it was not considered remarkable that an aged one should pass away. But then a robust and healthy young man fell dead for no perceivable reason; and every few weeks after that a member of the Long Salt family would become ill, begin to waste away, then die in suffering. To the more wise and astute members of the family it was becoming increasingly clear that someone had set a *chindi,* an evil spirit upon them. But why?

At last the lazy ones confessed their duplicity in substituting the antelope for the mutton. Family leaders of the Long Salts, who at that time numbered more than a hundred members, met in council to decide how best to deal with the frightening matter of a family curse. It was agreed that a party of Long Salts would meet with the medicine man and confront the situation without further delay.

The blind medicine man admitted that he had become angry when he discovered the deception that had been worked upon him by the Long Salts. He also admitted that he had set a chindi against the Long Salts with the instructions that the entire family should be exterminated.

The headmen of the Long Salts beseeched the medicine man to grant them a reprieve and to recall the evil demon. They had been duped as well as he by those loutish members of their family. Already several Long Salts had died. Surely he would not consider himself avenged for such a simple matter as five sheep.

The medicine man was touched by their pleas. He told them that he was not an evil man, but he had been forced to uphold his dignity and his reputation. He would remove the curse for a price, but at the moment he had no idea what to charge them for his services in recalling the chindi. He bade them return in ten days.

The delegation from the Long Salts were prompt in keeping their appointment, and on the morning of the tenth day they arrived before the hogan of the blind medicine man. They were greeted by a sober family in mourning. The medicine man had passed to the land of the spirits during the interim.

To the Long Salts' horror, they were unable to determine whether or not the medicine man had recalled the chindi before his unexpected death. By the time they reached home, however, they had their answer. Several members of the family lay ill and dying.

John R. Winslowe wrote (*Frontier Times,* August-September 1967) that he met the last surviving member of the Long Salts, a slender teen-aged girl named Alice, in 1925.

"Despite annual additions by births," Winslowe said, "the number of Long Salts steadily declined. By 1900 only ten were living. Long since they had despaired of the family's survival.

"Alice Long Salt was born in 1912. There were then only five of the family remaining, and all were young. They were her parents, two uncles and an aunt. Curiously, anyone marrying into the family met the same fate as a blood Long Salt. Alice's mother died when the girl reached seven and while she was attending the Tuba City boarding school at the Indian agency. Alice's father became skin and bones, dying two years later. That left her an orphan. The remaining three Long Salts were ill, crippled and helpless. Friends cared for them, watching them fade into nothing before their eyes."

By 1925, Alice's uncles and aunt had succumbed to the chindi's attack and she was the last of the Long Salts. The teen-ager had been the top student in her class at the agency school, but within a few months of the death of the last of her relatives, her teachers noticed Alice becoming dull and listless. Soon she was ill with a malady that defied the medical doctors' conventional methods of diagnosis.

An aging but determined man named Hosteen Behegade adopted Alice Long Salt and resolved that he would protect the girl from the chindi's efforts to destroy the sole surviving member of a family that had sought to deceive a blind old medicine man. Although Behegade was considered rather well off with a respectable number of sheep, horses, and cattle, medicine men conducted their sings free of charge. Each earnestly desired to be the one whose medicine could thwart the demon, but they privately admitted that they knew their attempts would come to nothing.

"By late 1927," Winslowe continued the story, "Behegade had expended all his property and was heavily in debt, fighting bravely for the girl's life.

"That year Behegade evolved a plan. To finish off the stricken girl the *chindi* had to be present. His idea was to keep moving constantly, concealing his trail. By this means he could prevent the *chindi* from locating Alice.

"One dark night an owl hooted close by. At dawn Alice Long Salt was too weak to leave her blankets. The *chindi* had found its innocent victim again. From then on Behegade always obeyed the owl's hoot, believing that it had come to his aid against the *chindi*."

In the winter of 1928, the fearful wanderers found themselves seeking refuge from a blizzard in a hogan three miles from the trading post on Red Mesa. Alice seemed to rally in health and she became cheerful. Perhaps the blizzard would protect them. Surely the chindi could not find them amidst the deep-piling snow and the howling wind.

The blizzard developed into the worst snowstorm in years. The Behegade family relaxed their guard and slept peacefully. Not even a chindi could combat such a violent working of the elements.

The next morning Alice Long Salt was dead. The final act of propitiation had been made. At last the chindi would return to whatever realm from whence it had come, its one hundred-year mission of vengeance completed.

Standing in full ritualistic attire, Iron Eyes Cody performs the Sun Dance. Below, he is shown ready to offer a solemn prayer to the gods as another brave is pierced during the ceremony. Cody is convinced that the power of the American Indian cannot be surpassed in matters of magic.

CHAPTER NINE

Indian Witchcraft

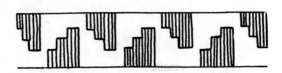

When one employs any form of energy, whether it be physical or spiritual, one is dealing with both positive and negative elements. Cursing, hexing, and the manipulation of familiar spirits are as well known in Amerindian medicine as they are in the traditions of European magic. Native American practitioners of this personally exploitive and malignly directed medicine are as feared and respected as the village witch or *Hexenmeister* in European culture.

Since I recognize Wicca as a legitimate form of religious expression that has nothing whatsoever to do with dark, satanic evil, I share the dismay of my many Craft friends who object to the designation of "Witch" being applied to practitioners of magical systems which endeavor to control malignant psychic or spirit forces in order to achieve personal gain or personal vengeance. But, alas, due to semantic limitations, I, too, in order to facilitate communication between author and reader, am often forced into using the term "Witch" to differentiate the manipulators of bad medicine from those whose medicine remains a personal, or tribally shared, vision.

It should really come as no surprise that the Witches of European tradition are most sympathetic toward Amerindian medicine in particular, and to the social plight of the Amerindian in general. The American-Sicilian Magus Dr. Leo Louis Martello told me:

The moral leukemia practiced by the white man against the red man, wherein the white corpuscles eat up the red ones, can only result in the weakening and spiritual death of the white man. This cancer of conscience of the U.S. Government has resulted in the total demoralization and dehumanization of both its perpetrators and its victims.

As a Witch, as a Pagan, as an advocate of individual rights; as a public supporter of all liberation movements (though not necessarily their motives or methods); as an American citizen; as one who lives by a three-word life philosophy (value for value); as one who foresaw and wrote about the rise of Red Power in 1960; as one who identifies with Nature, the natural, the rational; as a member of a minority religion; as one who has applauded man's technological achievements, but who has always identified with, and used, true magic; as one who has never claimed to be an altruist, but a practitioner of moral selfishness (i.e., everyone has the right to pursue his own best interests as long as they are not at the expense of another); my complete support of the Amerindian is not based on pity or a sense of false superiority, but on the recognition of his value as a human being, a blood

75

brother, a fellow pagan, who has been cruelly oppressed, but who is now rediscovering his own valid life-style and his own creative culture. This process of rediscovery will free the Indian of trying to be a Plastic Patriot or a carbon copy of the white man. The American Indian will once again manifest himself in the manifold magic of the Great Spirit.

The U.S. Constitution stresses freedom of religion, yet the humanitarian Christian missionaries crushed the spiritual heritage of the Amerindian. In place of his soul, they offered him a bowl of soup; they replaced his Happy Hunting Ground with a Christian Hell, his bow with a cross. And he has been spiritually crucified ever since. If the American Indian is to fully regain his self-identity, then he must reject conquering Christianity. He must reject the charge that he was a "pagan" or a "heathen" in need of conversion. He was/is a pagan of the country in its most profoundly positive sense.

The Amerindian must learn to uproot any sense of inferiority fostered on him by the conquering Christian white man. He must be certain that he has not accepted the white's evaluation of himself, even on a subconscious level. He must not judge himself by Caucasian technological progress.

The United States, unlike other countries, is not based on a geographical accident, but on an ideal. Until those in power uphold this ideal, right the wrongs, grant to the indigenous peoples the same rights it claims for itself, this country will never be at peace.

The Resurrection of the Great Spirit will succeed because it is based on justice, on unassailable rightness, on irrefutable facts. The Wheel of Fortune has turned. Mighty Manitou will replace the Mighty Machine. The ancient gods and goddesses have come out of their hibernation. The long sleep is over. Manitou and the Mighty Ones of all ancient faiths are now claiming their own.

The basics of cursing one's victim to death seem to follow general principles of application, regardless of whether the practitioner performs his grim art in Polynesia, Paris, or the plains of Kansas. the Kahuna, Witch, or Medicine Man utilizes the physical stimulus of an image or a picture of the enemy to achieve an altered state of consciousness which permits him to manifest controlled psychokinesis—the direct action of mind on matter. The "voodoo doll," the clay image, the mud ball that contains bits of the victim's hair or nail parings have no function in the malign magical transference, other than to serve as a physical stimulus upon which the practitioner may direct his conscious thoughts. Meditation upon such an artifact provides an impetus for the psyche's bursting free of the body's inhibiting three-dimensional bonds and developing the awesome power to, prismlike, focus enough psychic energy to affect the physical and mental functioning of the confused enemy.

Other researchers, who may not recognize such non-physical capacities of man, generally theorize that the intended victim gains knowledge of the curse and literally scares himself to death. Anthropologist Walter Cannon spent several years collecting examples of "voodoo death," instances in which men and women died as a result of having been the recipients of curses, alleged supernatural visitations, or societal taboos.

Since fear, one of the most powerful and deep-rooted of the emotions, has its effects mediated through the nervous system and the endocrine apparatus, the sympathetic adrenal system, Cannon hypothesized that, "if these powerful emotions prevail and the bodily forces are fully mobilized for action, and if this state of extreme perturbation continues for an uncontrolled possession of the organism for a considerable period ... dire results my ensue."

Cannon suggested, then, that "voodoo death" may result from a state of shock due to a persistent and continuous outpouring of adrenaline and a depletion of the adrenal corticosteroid hormones. Such a constant agitation caused by an abiding sense of fear could consequently induce a fatal reduction in blood pressure. Cannon assessed "voodoo death" as a real phenomenon set in motion by "shocking emotional stress—to obvious or repressed terror."

In his collection of case histories of individuals who had willed others, or themselves, to death (*Scared To Death*), Dr. J.C. Barker assessed voodoolike death as "resulting purely from extreme fear and exhaustion ... essentially a psychosomatic phenomenon." In his opinion, in those cases in which deaths result from premonitions, predictions, and curses, the victims died from autosuggestion. Dr. Baker states: "Initially the subject develops the notion that something is going to happen; then this idea operates through autosuggestion so as to bring about the very thing which was anticipated. We have already become familiar with the powerful consequences of suggestion, which can have particularly harmful effects upon the subject's state of health. It would be difficult to dismiss the death (in a particular case he cites) as being due to natural causes. If death was occasioned by other agencies, they were certainly not apparent."

77

My response to such hypotheses as the above is to remark that knowledge of a curse may certainly *help* bring about its unpleasant fruition, but such knowledge is by no means necessary if an accomplished practitioner has focused his psychic prism upon a victim. I am aware of too many cases wherein the suffering victims were totally unaware on a conscious level that a curse had been levied against them, and I have had too many acquaintances in the missionary and medical fields relate accounts of their utter helplessness when attempting to aid someone who was later discovered to have been cursed.

I personally have had the experience of having an external intelligence direct my selection of cards from a deck, my choice of numbers to be written on a note pad, and, in one case, even my behavior and my conversation. Fortunately, I was being controlled—not against my will, but without my knowledge—by Olof Jonsson, who is not only a master psychic sensitive, but one of the most saintlike men I have ever known.

After recounting incidents wherein Olof mentally directed a bus driver to turn around in the middle of the street, convinced a thief to return his stolen loot, and, in Australia, directed a politician to speak against himself and to endorse his opponent, I wrote in *The Psychic Feats of Olof Jonsson:* "It is rather frightening if one really considers the implications of this strange facet of 'psi,' this 'telepathic-psychokinesis,' or whatever it may be. Perhaps there exist other masters of this awesome talent who are not as jovial and benign as Olof Jonsson. Maybe, down through the ages, this has been what black magic, voodoo, and hexing have really been all about—the genuine ability of one mind to affect the thoughts and the behavior patterns of another. Psychokinesis, the direct action of mind upon matter or mind upon mind, may be the real power behind what superstition and ignorance have termed the 'Black Arts.'"

But we have not discussed the type of cursing which involves chindis, demons, familiar spirits. When I am more disposed toward a process of psychokinetic projection explaining curses and "voodoo death," I will not deny that there may well be forces or intelligences which may be harnessed—and at least partially controlled—by particularly powerful adepts. These Nature entities (for lack of a better term) may represent another order of intelligence which somehow shares our planet with us, or they may be but another manifestation of the life-force, the Spirit, that pervades every living thing. In either event, I feel confident that I may present generalized principles by which the practitioner—Witch, Kahuna, Medicine Man—curses with spirits.

The practitioner is one who had attained a high level in his craft. He has studied under a great master, and he has either been given, or has acquired as a result of his own intense efforts, a familiar spirit or spirits.

When a person is to be prayed to death (i.e., cursed) for any one of numerous reasons, the practitioner summons his familiar spirits and begins the ceremony of instruction. In many cases, the spirits will be propitiated with an offering of food, for it is believed that the entities will absorb spirit force (called *orenda* by many Amerindian tribes, but *mana* most commonly in a kind of metaphysical consensus) from the victuals which the practitioner has surrounded with ceremonial objects.

The familiar spirits, their strength intensified by mana, are now provided with explicit instructions. They are commanded to catch a scent from a bit of hair or a soiled garment belonging to the enemy, and they are told to follow it as a hunting dog sniffs a game track. Once they have definitely located the victim, they are to await an opportune moment to enter his body and absorb his vital force. The practitioner chants his instructions over and over, not only providing the familiar spirits with an image of the victim, but supplementing their power with direct charges from his own psyche.

The Kahuna, Witch, Medicine Man believes that the spirits enter the body of the intended victim, or attach themselves to it, and vampirelike, absorb his vital force and store it in their own ghostly bodies. As the mana of the enemy is withdrawn, a numbness comes over him, which generally begins at the feet and rises slowly over a period of three days to knees, hips, and finally to the heart. Once the numbness has encircled the heart, the enemy will soon be dead.

When the victim has expired, the satiated spirits withdraw,.taking with them their newly absorbed charges of mana. Upon their return to their master, the practitioner, they are commanded to play about the lodge until they have dissipated the vital force which they have stolen from the victim. Such spirit recreation finds its release in poltergeistic activities, in which objects are tossed about in violent explosions of energy.

If the intended victim should be rescued through the paranormal prowess of another practitioner, the invading spirits might be directed to the one who chants the death prayer with fatal results. In order to prevent such a boomerang of the death curse, the skilled practitioner who looks for longevity in his craft will always observe a ritual cleansing. In certain cases, the more cautious practitioners will demand that the person who has employed them to send out a curse take an oath that the named victim is truly deserving of such drastic punishment. Should another practitioner, or the spiritual strength of the intended victim himself, thereby accomplish a reversal of the curse, the client alone will be held accountable by the enraged familiar spirits.

Universal metaphysical law seems to have it that no practitioner, no matter how skilled or adept, no matter how long he has fasted or purged himself, may direct a curse against an innocent victim without suffering a reversal of the death prayer upon himself. If the outraged spirits do not boomerang upon him at once, they will almost assuredly return to work their ruin on him after they have accomplished the unjust deed which they were sent to do.

Such, it is believed, was the case when Maman-ti, the Owl Prophet, chanted the death prayer for the powerful Kiowa chief Kicking Bird.

The Owl Prophet is not to be portrayed as a sinister practitioner of medicine. He was esteemed by his own Kiowa people and was so highly regarded by those tribes with which the Kiowa held alliances that the Comanches named him to the position of master of all medicine men. He has been described as a tall, aristocratic man, a warrior-priest who not only fought in the important battles but who led raids of strategic value.

Maman-ti, He-Who-Touches-the-Sky, earned the appellation of Owl Prophet because it was the owl that became his totem-familiar spirit and would come to tell the medicine man the outcome of future battles. While the council chiefs sat in silence, Maman-ti would listen to the screeching cries of an owl sounding from somewhere in the darkness. There would be the beating of wings, an interlude of silence while Maman-ti sat in meditation, then the Owl Prophet would interpret the message from his familiar.

By 1875 the Kiowas and their allies had been battered, scattered, and defeated by the white men with their inexhaustible supplies of men, weapons, and ammunition. Many of the war leaders were dead. Five years before, the great chief Kicking Bird had assessed their situation as futile and had urged large numbers of Kiowa and members from the allied tribes to save their lives and join him in the settlement outside of Fort Sill, Oklahoma. Only Lone Wolf, the Owl Prophet and a few others headed small bands that continued to wage a guerrilla warfare against the numerically superior Blue Coats. Then, in February, Kicking Bird managed to convince even these determined defenders of their land to break their arrows and set aside their rifles.

Quite understandably, Kicking Bird was regarded with contempt by those of his people who had vowed to fight until the last man. For five years he had lived with his family in a comfortable lodge near a white man's fort, while his friends and allies maintained a war that was as much his responsibility to support. Even so, since Kicking Bird had his people's best interests at heart and had been compelled to make his decisions according to his medicine, some kind of union between the factions might have been accomplished if General Sherman had not decreed that certain of the recently surrendered Indians must be punished for their recalcitrance. The military authorities soon found themselves in a quandary as they attempted to decide which of their prisoners should be most eligible for imprisonment, so they turned the disagreeable affair over to Kicking Bird and told him to select twenty-six Kiowas for banishment to the dungeons of Fort Marion, Florida.

Kicking Bird complied with the orders from the military authorities. He chose Long Wolf, the Owl Prophet, Woman's Heart, and White Horse—because of their repeated raids into Texas—then rounded out the remainder of the quota with a random selection of warriors and a few Mexican captives who had been reared with the allied tribes. Although he had obeyed the white man's dictum with a heavy heart, now many of Kicking Bird's most loyal followers had come to regard him as a traitor and a self-aggrandizing opportunist.

On April 28, as the chained prisoners were being loaded into wagons for the long trip to Florida, Kicking Bird rode up and told the Kiowas how much he had regretted his part in their exile.

"I am sorry," he said, "but because of your stubbornness, you have not kept out of trouble. You will have to be punished by the government. It will not be for long. I love you and will work for your release."

The Kiowas in their chains, contemplating imprisonment in a foreign climate, were little impressed with Kicking Bird's sentiments and his promise to work for their parole.

Maman-ti had not lost his ability as an orator, and he delivered a scornful diatribe toward the chief he considered a traitor. He said that although Kicking Bird might be a big man among the whites and might remain free in his luxurious lodge, he should cherish his every moment of life. One day, the Owl Prophet promised, he would kill him.

81

Two days later on the journey, Eagle Chief, a medicine man of high ability, managed to find a seat near Maman-ti.

"You promised to kill Kicking Bird with your hands," Eagle Chief reminded him. "You have the medicine to kill him from a great distance."

"The death prayer?"

Eagle Chief nodded.

The Owl Prophet sat for several moments without speaking another word; then he said, "You know my medicine forbids me to use it against a Kiowa. It has been revealed to me that I, too, would die if I were to sing the death prayer for one of my people."

"Will there be life for you in a Florida prison?" Eagle Chief asked him.

The Owl Prophet said no more. Eagle Chief interpreted his silence as withdrawal and he turned away from his tribesman, fearful that he had asked too much.

The wagons were quiet for many hours; then the Kiowas heard the keening wail of the death prayer.

Two mornings later, after drinking a cup of coffee, the robust, healthy, forty-year-old Kicking Bird collapsed in great pain. He died just before noon, while the agency doctor stood helplessly at his bedside.

The Owl Prophet uttered a sigh of resignation when the wagonloads of prisoners received word that Kicking Bird was dead. He would endure the discomforts of travel willingly. The dungeons of Fort Marion held no threat for him. By the end of the journey, the Owl Prophet had died of "natural causes," according to the official report.

One may theorize about poison in Kicking Bird's coffee—as did the agency doctor; one may hypothesize that the Owl Prophet willed himself to death on a subconscious level; but you should not be surprised if you are unable to find a medicine adept who will accept either supposition.

"Among ourselves we are not afraid to admit that we still believe in ghosts and witches and things of this nature, because we know that we are not going to be laughed at," Don Wilkerson told me.

"I know some people might say that we are old-fashioned, but that doesn't bother us too much. I would be reticent to tell a lot of people that ghosts and witches are very much a part of our everyday life. We have good and bad witches, and although you won't find too many Indian people admitting to this in the cities, you will find it very much a part of life at home on the reservation. There are many cleansing ceremonies to take care of evil influences. Reams of incantations have been written in the Cherokee language to deal with evil. We are talking about something real—not superstition or psychiatric problems."

Gavin Frost, Director of the School of Wicca, is not only sympathetic toward the rebirth of Amerindian medicine power, he is convinced that the many similarities between European Witchcraft and Indian magic indicate that the aboriginal peoples of America received instruction in Wicca from early Celtic practitioners of the Craft.

Gavin Frost: *In order to understand a little of the Wicca way, you have to delve somewhat into Celtic, and specifically Welsh and Irish, mythology. These mythologies all start from what is often known as the Ancient Ones, or the* Previlt. *These Ancient Ones always live in large cities, which the Welsh tradition calls* Dinasassaraon, *the place of the higher powers. The headquarters in Wales was in* Dinas Emerys *(literally, City of the Dragons of Bel) in the Mountains of Snowdon.*

The first great Celtic goddess is Cerridwen, who learned her art from the Ancient Ones in the ridge city, an exceedingly strong fortification encompassed by a circular, triple wall. The carriage of Cerridwen was drawn by dragons, and she had several magical items which always went with her.

Gavin and Yvonne Frost.
Bishops in the Church and
School of Wicca, in New Bern, North Carolina

The most important was the Cauldron of Inspiration. This has recently been equated with the Holy Grail, because it is a vessel which contains all of the life fluids—one drop of which will give you inspiration. We also have to equate the Cauldron with the Indians' Sacred Pipe, in which sweet grasses were smoked to encourage astral flight.

The second item Cerridwen had was a stone of knowledge. A stone that knew everything.

Then she had certain animals—the white sow, the young wolf, and the young eagle.

The tradition in Welsh Craft circles is that about A.D. 800 to 1000, Witches left the coast of Wales and traveled across the sea. These people were searching for mountains similar to their own where they could hide out from the onslaught and onrush of the new religion of Christianity. They navigated by fixed sights on the boat. They were excellent astronomers. They had no difficulty finding a land as large as North America.

There were, in all, a complete coven of twelve in the first group, and the Indians on the eastern coast respected their power. This first coven taught all those who would come to them. Twelve more migrations took place, the last being about 1600. The people of the last migration stayed together and became those whom we now refer to as the Robed Ones of the Ozarks. In recent times we have contacted some of these people, and we have found that their rituals are like ours in almost every detail.

The intermediate migrations—the first group and the last group stayed together, remember—traveled throughout the land giving freely of their knowledge. I would like to look at some of the Amerindian traditions and show you how they received their bases.

Most of the Indian tribes recall the White Buffalo Woman, the white Witch who came from the East to give them power and knowledge. Throughout the Indian people there is the persistent myth of the Lost White Brother, the white people who were coming and who would come later.

Of course the Witches thought that they would be followed by a large migration of people from Wales, so they were preparing their Indian friends for all these other white people who would be coming across the ocean. That the extensive immigration didn't happen is, of course, partially due to the fact that Christianity did not take on in the hills of Wales as fast as the Witches feared it would; and, secondly, at least in the early days of Christianity, there was no insistence on the Wicca giving up their pagan ways, so the people of the Craft gradually got used to their new lives, rather than the persecution that the Witches had been expecting.

The White Buffalo Woman [a Celtic High Priestess of Wicca] brought with her the pipe of inspiration, the sacred pipe. She brought with her a stone, and she told them that three animals were sacred—the white buffalo, the young coyote, and the young eagle.

The sacred pipe has on it twelve spotted eagle feathers, in remembrance that the eagle is sacred. The bowl of the pipe, of course, is stone, in remembrance of the stone of knowledge.

It seems that the White Buffalo Woman did not have a white sow with her, so she substituted the white buffalo.

If you look at a typical sweathouse ceremony of the American Indians, you will find that they sit in a circle with a fire in the center. They put up four posts in the four quadrants, or toward the four points of the compass, and they have the door to the east. This is an exact replica of the initial stages of building a Witches' circle.

We put up four candles, which have often been called the watchtowers, in the four quadrants. We have our gate in our circle to the east, where people can enter; and we always have, when we are outside at least, a simple fire in the center of the circle. I do not think there exists this similarity of arrangement by chance.

Perhaps one of the most interesting things that we have found in our research of the similarities between the Wicca way and the Amerindian tradition is the labyrinth. To a Witch, the Cretan labyrinth is a most important symbol, for it signifies the various steps you have to go through in order to reach the Cauldron of Inspiration.

The Cauldron of Inspiration can be reached only after laboriously tracing every path of a seven-tiered labyrinth. Our ancient tradition says that a child will willingly follow all of the paths and get to the center, whereas an adult will always try to find a quicker way—and discover that there is no quicker way. One must cover the whole of the labyrinth in order to reach the Cauldron of Inspiration in the center. ["Except one become as a child" is an oft-repeated dictum in Western mysticism and in the Christian tradition, as well as in the mystery schools.]

If you were to look in The Book of the Hopi by Frank Waters, Part One, Chapter Five, you will see two Earth Mother symbols; and you will see there a representation of the labyrinth. This is the same labyrinth that appears on rock carvings at Tintagel, King Arthur's castle. It is the labyrinth that is found at Glastonbury. [For the Hopi, the squared maze design represents spiritual rebirth from one world to another and is known as Tapu'at, Mother and Child. The circular type signifies the Road of Life which man must follow in order to reach the center and be guaranteed rebirth.]

Glastonbury is the "glass town that is buried," the other world of the Celtic religion. The spiral castle is also interestingly found in Hopi legend in the corkscrew manner in which one must go down, or come up, from the other world. When we compare the Hopi symbol we see that it is an exact representation of the Cretan labyrinth, but it is a mirror image. It is reversed.

The crooked cross, although often thought of as a Hopi symbol, is the reverse of the double S—the intertwined S. The double S was Christianized into Sancto Spiritus, but to us of the Wicca, the symbol means Spirit and Soul—the two being tied together so tightly as to be inseparable. We do not understand why these things were mirrored, but I find it interesting the way these things come out.

There are so many other similarities between Wicca and Amerindian traditions that it is difficult to choose which ones to discuss. The man going on his vision quest, various initiation ceremonies, the rites of purification—all of these ceremonies and observances were held at the full of the moon. All of these things are the same.

The word wakan, which is one of the words in the secret language used for "holy or sacred," correctly means "power." One continually comes across the word wakan in many Amerindian tribes, and one should think of it in terms of meaning power, rather than sacredness. This same word is also found in Islam, spelled Waqt—an interesting similar spelling.

Then there are the ceremonial dances. The suwise or clockwise circumambulation is always used by the Sioux. Occasionally, however, the counterclockwise movement is used in a dance of some occasion prior to, or after, a great catastrophe. The counterclockwise movement is an imitation of the thunder beings who always act in an anti-natural way. This is precisely what the Wicca do when they want to heal or to help—they work in a clockwise, or deosil manner. When they want to harm or to prevent an ugly thing from happening, they work in the witichins, or anti-clockwise manner.

Manitou, who in the sacred language is called Skan, is an all-pervasive, ever-present, unnamed being—and, I should say, not even a being, because *the concept does not take on any humanistic or animalistic form. It is there. It is present. It is everywhere.*

Now, the traditional Indian beliefs maintain that all things have spirit—animals, plants, rocks—everything that is separable has a spirit within. The Wicca changed away from that concept, as far as I can tell, around A.D. 500. I don't know why they changed away from it, but they turned to the belief that every living thing has a spirit, that inanimate objects do not have spirits. The Cauldron of Inspiration gave one the capability of contacting the spirits of all living things.

Another thing that the Wicca used to do, but changed away from about A.D. 500, was the trapping of spirits. The Wicca used to be very concerned with keeping the spirits of their ancestors around them so that they could be certain that the spirits were happy. At some point in time, around A.D. 500, they changed and they began, gradually at first, to consider that the spirit must go on and must be released to be happy. The Indian burial procedures and the manner in which they regard their ancestors all point, in my opinion, to their belief in the keeping of spirits around them. I think that the Amerindians received the earlier vision of Wicca, and that they have kept alive many Craft beliefs in their own traditions.

Have the Amerindians kept alive the ways of the Celtic Witches and incorporated the legends of immigrating Wicca covens into their own native traditions? Or do these similarities between the ways of Wicca and the ways of the Amerindian give but further evidence to the suggestion that there is something universal in man's spiritual evolution on this planet that prompts him to duplicate in substance "...what other groups of men in other natural settings have found to be *the human* truth, so that Aryan and Dakota, Greek and Pawnee, build identical ritual patterns to express their separate discoveries of a single insight"?

During the course of my research, I had the opportunity to speak with a delightful woman of Shawnee-Cherokee ancestry who has been a practicing rainmaker for twenty-five years. Ann Underwood of Beckley, West Virginia, underwent her training as a medicine person with her own grandfather serving as tutor. [At the time of our interview, she was the only individual of whom I had knowledge who was a practitioner of both Amerindian medicine and Celtic Wicca.] At the same time, Ann is very much aware of the universal aspects of her work, as well as being well informed in regard to certain parapsychological explanations for her medicine. All things considered, she was an excellent interviewee with whom to discuss magic, Witchcraft, and Indian medicine.

Ann Underwood: *I got roundly chastised by my mother the first time she caught me performing rain prayers for our garden that was drying out. She wasn't aware of the fact that my grandfather had taught me the Shawnee weather ritual, which he had learned from his mother; and I wasn't old enough to know that our white neighbors would frown on us if they saw me performing the rain ritual. I got switched for my efforts.*

In your opinion, what is the power that makes rain rituals work?

Mrs. Underwood: *Oh well, it is not the dance and it is not the chant. It isn't the fire or what is offered to the fire. It is the prayers of the Great Spirit to the Mystery to send rain to prevent the crops from failing. The Indians depended for their staples on their crops. Hunting was a little chancy at the best of times, so it was their food crops that keep them alive. They prayed for rain when they needed it.*

There was a need; it was asked to be fulfilled, and the need was met.

Mrs. Underwood: *The Indians painted their faces with the symbol of rain, but not of lightning. They took natural water and moistened the end of their prayer sticks and drove them into the ground with one thrust. They painted the rain symbol around the ceremonial fire. This was symbolic ritual.*

The main thing was that the shamans would dance, chant, and focus their thoughts, their prayers.

Sending an impulse to the Great Spirit.

Mrs. Underwood: *Yes, for hours and hours sometimes—until it worked or the last shaman had danced himself into exhaustion.*

Do you think the sacrifice element was necessary—the offering of tobacco and food—or was this act in the nature of physical stimulus for the prayers?

Mrs. Underwood: *I think the sacrifice was just a focal point for individual thought, a concentration point, like a mandala.*

I believe that Amerindian traditional beliefs are very similar to the Paleolithic religions of Europe and Asia. Ivar Lissner [Man, God, and Magic] brings out the theory that man has always been monotheistic. Since we are supposed to have come across the Bering Strait, I think we brought this religion with us. When we lost contact with the other continents, we altered the religion, of course, but, basically, it is still the same religion.

For example, the ceremonial fires are kindled in the same way. The horned mask or headdress of the shaman, the medicine man, is the same (I prefer the term shaman to medicine man, having been a shaman for twenty-five years).

As a shaman, how are you asked to serve people in your particular locale?

Mrs. Underwood: *I deal primarily with weather rituals. Weather can be a terrible problem here. We have a saying in West Virginia that we have "too weather." We either have too much or too little. Either we have had a constant downpour for the last three years, or we have had a prolonged drought for the last six years. Either we don't have enough snow to keep the soil from being weather-killed, or else we have three feet of snow all at once. So I am mainly asked to help control things in our part of the state.*

Would you care to give an estimate of your percentage of effectiveness?

Mrs. Underwood: *Oh, I think I can safely say about 70 per cent.*

Could you tell us something about your training for the role of shaman?

Mrs. Underwood: *Well, I suppose Grandpa had been instructing me in the delicate art of weather control for about two years before—at age twelve—I fasted for a week, then slept out in the woods to await my vision. Then I went back to Grandpa and told him what I had seen. We had our own private celebration, and I was able to study and to practice medicine seriously.*

One usually thinks of a shaman as being male.

Mrs. Underwood: *It didn't make any difference in our tribe whether the shaman was male or female. If you had the qualifications which indicated that you could possibly be a shaman, it did not matter if you were male or female—you would be accepted for training and taught. The final test was what you saw after you had undergone the period of fasting, the ritual baths of cold water, and the time of waiting for the vision.*

Grandfather had been initiated into shamanship by his mother. He had no sons, so there had to be a gap of a generation before he could initiate a granddaughter. You see, among the Shawnee medicine people, knowledge passes in the same manner as it does among the Wicca. Females can only teach males. Males can only teach females. And you must learn those rituals—which are often very complicated—letter perfect!

Another criterion appears to be that you must have had what they called the "falling sickness" sometime during your life. By this, of course, is meant a violent convulsion due to a high fever, epilepsy, or some other cause. I had one fairly violent convulsion from a food allergy—I have a vague idea it was from blackberries—that made me eligible.

So this allergy produced convulsions, your grandfather observed you in this condition, and it gave him the first of a series of signs that you could qualify to study medicine.

Mrs. Underwood: *Yes, that is correct. He never taught my older sister.*

Do you induce visions so that you might guide others and yourself?

Mrs. Underwood: *I practice meditation, which amounts to the same thing.*

Do you have any difficulties incorporating Wicca with your traditional beliefs?

Mrs. Underwood: *No, I can't see where there is any conflict with Wicca.*

I have, though, tried two or three different Christian churches, and I found that I could not accept their teachings. In my opinion, their views conflicted with everything that I had been taught as a child. I grew up on the river and in the woods and received most of my traditional instruction from my grandparents. The traditional belief was always present in my mother, even though she didn't approve of my making rain rituals in front of our white neighbors.

What are you most concerned about in your medicine work today?

Mrs. Underwood: *I am most concerned about the carelessness and greed that man is showing toward our natural resources. We Indians never fight Nature. We would rather move with Nature. I think a respect for the Earth Mother is born in nearly all of us. We are taught that the Earth belongs to the Great Spirit, to God. It doesn't belong to us. It is only ours to use for a little while. We must not mistreat it or abuse it, because it must be passed on to the next generation.*

I am very deeply grieved to see men so greedy. I sometimes feel like unbraiding my hair, gashing my arms, spreading ashes on my face, and chanting a wail of sorrow.

As further evidence of the universality of psychic, supernatural, and mythic experience, the Amerindian's cosmology is not devoid of night creatures, horrid things of darkness—all the denizens of nightmares that haunt men and women of all cultures.

"The wolfmen are not werewolves, mind you, but wolves or men or supernatural beings that take the shape of men and—at will—can travel many, many miles in the wink of an eye and appear as wolves or as men dressed in wolf's clothing, so to speak," Don Wilkerson told me. "Now, you won't tell an Indian that these things do not happen. If you get among the Navajo, you might find someone who will tell you of these things."

"One evening my brother was going to my grandmother's. It was late at night, and he was on a dirt road hitchhiking," said the attractive young Navajo woman. She was a secretary in Phoenix, a convert to Roman Catholicism.

"It was in February, and it was pretty cold. It was past midnight and he just couldn't go any farther. They have these little bus stops on the roads—you know, where they pick up schoolchildren—so he was just around there debating whether to spend the night in there or to keep walking the second half of the fifty miles to Grandmother's home.

"Then he saw this animal. He thought it was a dog. He wanted some company so he whistled at it. It came running right by him and they scared each other. The 'dog' stood up on its hind legs. My brother said it had a man's face, and the face was painted with little white dots and other kinds of signs. It had an animal's skin on. The thing ran off on four legs and my brother tried to run after it, but it was too fast.

"My brother said that it dawned on him then what he had seen. He had never really believed in things like that until then. He said, 'I guess it is true that medicine men really have the power to travel in that way.' In other words, medicine men have the power to travel long distances in no time at all in the form of a wolf. During the time that they are traveling in this fashion, they are not supposed to talk to anybody until they reach their destination.

"He did not tell my grandmother about the incident until several months later, because, if he had, my grandmother would get excited, you know, and she would say that we would have to have a *sing* to chase the evil spirits away. When he told us about his experience, it made us wonder about it."

In my opinion, true magic lies in the unlimited reach of the psyche: mind contacting mind through other than sensory means; mind influencing matter and other minds; mind elevating itself to a level of consciousness where past, present and future become an Eternal Now. Although man may clothe these experiences according to the cultural context in which he is most functional, these evidences of man's non-physical capabilities are universal.

I believe that prestidigitation, the-hand-is-quicker-than-the-eye kind of magic, was born when man began to use his *brain* in an attempt to mimic the transcendental qualities of his *mind*.

A canny young man, jealous of a shaman's ability to move an object through psychokinesis, mind influencing matter, retreats to a darkened lodge and duplicates the feat by attaching one end of a long black hair to a pebble and the other to a finger. Since the medicine person may have spent years acquiring the discipline requisite to a semi-controlled functioning of his "psi" ability and still cannot guarantee success on every attempt, the canny young man, who can guarantee results on every attempt if one will but step into his darkened lodge, will soon be capturing more than his share of the audience and more than his share of their fees for shamanistic services rendered.

In every expression of magic, there are two basic kinds—the genuine manifestation of controlled "psi" ability and an imitative exploitation based on the essence of the authentic.

It is the wise person who learns that the "magic" of spiritual blessings has been dispensed to all men.

It is the adept practitioner who learns, in quiet moments of meditation, how best to permit a stream of the great light of the Cosmos to reach in and enrich his soul and open the borders of the Unknown.

It is the recipient of Illumination who achieves a dramatic spiritual linkup with the powers within his own psyche and the blessed Harmony that governs the Universe.

"I have had my own experiences," Don Wilkerson admitted. "I have practiced medicine, and I still do. Although I am assimilated into society, I don't accept society for what it is. I work in it, but I don't live in it. I live in my own group. When I get home, society is left behind me. I am in my own world and my own thoughts.

"This does present a problem at times. I have heard many non-Indian people say that I am anti-social, but that is not the case. This is a protective device that many of us Indians employ. I have had to use it in order to survive.

"I was raised on the reservation, speaking the language, practicing all the traditions. Then I went through a lot of traumatic experiences trying to find myself in the world. I never really found anything that answered my needs, other than with my own people and my own religion.

"Close, non-physical, ESP-types of relationships develop among many in our Indian groups. My mother and I were always in communication on this level, and I could tell when she wanted me. We always knew how the other was feeling, even when I traveled all over the world. During my twenty-three years in the Army, I never once wrote to my mother, yet we were always in contact with one another on this level of consciousness. These things are common among the Indian people.

"The fact that many Indian people have developed this ability to such a high degree can cause them some problems when they are working in white society. They may up and leave to go home without notifying anyone, because they know that something is wrong and that it requires their immediate attention. It becomes impossible to articulate these things to many non-Indian people."

We have these happenings in our non-Indian culture, as well. But we educate ourselves out of them. The Indian is not afraid to resume a more basic approach to these non-physical experiences. He does not attempt to rationalize these things, as a member of non-Indian society might.

"I think this may be true," Wilkerson said. "I don't know whether it is because of the rebirth of medicine power or not, but it seems that more and more Indians are encouraging, and responding to, these kinds of feelings. These things are not superstitions, but they exist as a very real part of our people's lives."

Proud of his heritage, Dallas Chief Eagle warns that Earth cannot sustain any more of man's abuse and thus, a Great Purification is due in order to balance out the planet once more.

CHAPTER TEN

The Legend Of
The White Buffalo

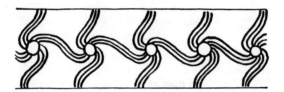

Every student of Amerindian culture has heard references to the legend of the White Buffalo. Occasionally, novels and motion pictures of frontier life will include scenes depicting the native peoples' "superstitious awe" of the sacred white buffalo. Here, for the first time, Dallas Chief Eagle has translated and shared the actual legend as it was set forth in the oral tradition of the Lakota people. The words are both powerful and beautiful in their simplicity, but do not be blocked from absorbing the universal and timeless relevance of the legend's message by the protective shield of pseudo-sophistication which modern man is supposed to have at the ready whenever he is exposed to "primitive myths." This legend has been repeated to countless generations as a teaching device. Do not be afraid to learn from wise ones who have long ago made their journey to the Spirit World.

* * *

My relation, I am an old man now, and I have seen many seasons file by like an animal procession to a water pond. Hear my tongue, my brother, for I have chosen this last sunset to tell you of an ancient legend. I feel the dawn will not follow the twilight of my life. When I sleep I will awake in the beyond, where there is no darkness.

This sacred legend had its beginning many winters before the Great Invasion from the dawn country. To ensure its continuation this legend is always handed down by men whose minds and eyes are wise and kind, men acquainted with sacred chants and meditations. This is why its exactness has never vanished. Being the present bearer, I hand down to you the "Legend of the White Buffalo." I hope your mind is ready to bind it for the next generation.

In an age before we had horses, in a season of budding spring, two braves went out scouting for the buffalo. For three days they hunted and tracked over plain, hill, and valley. On the fourth day, following the sunrise, the braves caught sight of a buffalo herd in a valley on the eastern stretch of the mountains. The herd was scattered across the valley.

The two hunters rushed their descent into the valley, and through habit of many hunts, slowed their pace as they neared the buffalo. Then it was, with equal surprise and joy, they noticed the white buffalo in the center of the herd. White with fur like winter etching, the prairie monarch stood motionless, enveloped in mystic vapor.

97

The hunters paused to robe themselves in wolf and coyote hides to kill their human odor, and readied their weapons. The buffalo throughout the valley began to move toward the White Buffalo, forming a circle around the White One. The two hunters moved cautiously toward an opening on the eastern side of the circle.

The music of nature does not fly in discord, and it was all around the valley. As the hunters crept closer to the opening in the herd, the spirit of the White Buffalo fully enveloped them, causing them to forget their desire to kill.

When the crouching hunters reached the opening, a blinding white flash brought them up straight. In place of the White Buffalo stood a beautiful woman in complete whiteness. In sunlight grandeur, she stood with hands extended, and the soft whisper of the wind made her hair, white skin, white robe, and white buckskin dress shimmer radiantly. Her mouth moved, and her voice, gentle and warm, flowed with a depth of sympathy that brought quiet to the valley.

I was here before the rains and the violent sea.
I was here before the snows and the hail.
I was here before the mountains and the winds.
I am the spirit of Nature.

I am in the light that fills the earth, and in the darkness of nighttime.
I give color to nature, for I am in nature's growth and fruits.
I am again in nature where themes of mystic wisdom are found.
I am in your chants and laughters.
I am in the tears that flow from sorrow.
I am in the bright joyous eyes of the children.

I am in the substance that gives unity, completeness, and oneness.
I am in the mountains as a conscious symbol to all mankind when earth's face is being scarred with spiritual undone.
I am in you when you walk the simple path of the red man.

I am in you when you show love of humankind, for I also give love to those who are loving.
I am in the response of love among all humans, for this is a path that will find the blessing and fulfillment of the Great Spirit.

I must leave you now to appear in another age, but I leave you with the red man's path.

Complete stillness was everywhere. The White Buffalo Spirit withdrew her hands, and with a glowing smile of eternal love, her body began to return to vapor.

One hunter could no longer contain himself from the beauty of the White Buffalo Spirit. His mind filled with extreme desire, he flung his weapons aside, brushed off his robe, and rushed for the fading spirit. A blinding flash again filled the circle. The White Buffalo Spirit was gone; the White Buffalo was gone; and all that remained was the skull of the charging hunter, gray ashes, and his formless bones.

This, my brother, is why we hold the White Buffalo to be sacred. The White Buffalo moves without the threat of an arrow or lance, whether we sight him in the northern forest, the plains country, or in the mountain regions.

I hope that your tongue can interpret the deep wisdom of this holy legend, and that you, my brother, may help to bring its message to all mankind.

Determining that their powwow powers should not be diminished with time,
Twylah Nitsch, like other Amerindians, are continuing to teach courses in
magic. Here, Twylah is seen in ceremonial dress
in a state of meditation.
(Photo credit Robert Koch).

CHAPTER ELEVEN

The Symbolism
Of Four

"Why is the number four sacred to the Amerindian?" I inquired of Twylah.

Remember when the four ancient ones ascended in the Light to the Great Mystery and saw the extended hand?

They learned that the symbolism of four was present in their extended hand; it meant life, unity, equality, and eternity. It also meant seeing, smelling, tasting, and hearing. These four senses could not function without feeling. Feeling includes touch and all emotion. When the hand is clasped, it is the symbol of unity. Unity is the spiritual law that binds the entire universe.

They descended with a feeling of being completely healed of all the thoughts they had that were not right. From this experience they saw how the Pathway of Peace should be followed and how the great lessons should be learned. They learned at this time that self-knowledge was the key; self-understanding was the desire; self-control was the way, and self-realization was the goal.

They discovered that everything goes in a circle, and that communication is the key to the pathway of learning. They learned communication means understanding; understanding means peace of mind; peace of mind leads toward happiness; therefore, happiness is communicating. A circle again!

And consider these symbolic representations of the number four:

The first four Creations were Sun, Moon, Water, Earth.
The four laws of Creation are life, unity, equality, eternity.
The four seasons are spring, summer, fall, winter.
The four directions are east, north, west, south.
The four races of Creation are white, red, yellow, black.
The four senses of feeling are seeing, hearing, tasting, smelling.
The four guidelines toward self-development are the following:
Am I happy doing what I am doing?
What am I doing to add to the confusion?
What am I doing to bring about peace and contentment?
How will I be remembered when I am gone—in absence and in death?
The four requirements of good health are food, sleep, cleanliness, good thoughts.
The four divisions of nature are spirit, mind, body, life.
The four divisions of goals are faith, love, work, pleasure.

103

The four ages of development are the learning age, the age of adoption, the age of improvement, the age of wisdom.

The four expressions of sharing are making others feel you care; an expression of interest (everything in creation has something to offer; listen and learn); an expression of friendship (promotes spiritual growth); an expression of belonging (sharing of goals toward a higher spiritual growth).

My grandfather, Moses Shongo, spent so much time breaking things down in fours. He taught me to do things in fours, and all my life I have done this. When I iron clothes, I iron in fours. I iron four things and put them away. Then four more. When I clean, I clean in fours. I don't do things this way, I don't feel good. If I don't satisfy myself in doing something, I don't bother doing it. It is amazing how it works.

Unity is the great spiritual law, and we can break that down into four parts, as well:

1. Unity is going into the Silence in spirit, mind, and body.

2. It is a union through which all spirituality flows.

3. It is a goal toward communicating with all things in nature.

4. It is recognized by the intellect through the senses, through the emotions, and through impressions.

Unity is the law of nature. I have known this since I can remember. Everything has its place, and everything works in unison. If you get in trouble, it is because you have created some static in this unified picture. You have only yourself to deal with. You only have control over yourself; therefore, you have to begin there. Equality to the Indian meant that everything in this universe had a place.

I could see no reason to disagree with her logical remarks, wise and educated is she in the ways of Indian magic.

Many native Hawaiians believe strongly that guardians spirits protect them, their loved ones, as well as their homes from negativity, and can bring them good luck. Such a spirit is seen here with arms raised to the heavens in front of a hut used by one of the original Kahuna High Priests to perform a sacred ritual.

(Photo by Timothy Green Beckley)

CHAPTER TWELVE

Kahuna Magic

The system of Huna was the power system of the Polynesian Islands at the advent of the white man and his religion. Western culture could not compete with the Kahuna priest on his own terms, so it instigated a program of limiting his practice, legally, through the political structure. In a little more than a generation the native Americans in Polynesia had overwhelmingly embraced western culture, along with its style of dress and its religion. There are few practicing Kahunas on the Islands today, but I have had opportunities to meet the ones I consider the most powerful.

I came in contact with Max Freedom Long in about 1968. He, of course, was the grand old man of Kahuna magic. He sent me package after package of books and tapes and notes and clippings, and he shared with me many of the secrets that he had accumulated in his research, which began at the turn of the century.

When I was first in Hawaii, in February of 1972, I was able to meet such Kahunas as Reverend Eddie Kung, who is the son of a Kahuna who had great healing powers; Sam Loma; and a woman of great power named Morna Simeona. I listened to tale after tale of how Kahuna magic had proved again and again to be too powerful for such modern mechanisms as sparkplugs and internal combustion engines. I heard how mysterious things would keep interfering with the work of the bulldozers of sacred grounds—how even state officials had grown impatient trying to confront the power of Kahuna priests.

Today most of the Kahunas have gone underground. There are a few who perform showy type rituals, just as in New Orleans there are Voodoo priests who do certain dances and certain rituals for the tourists. These performances are a kind of reflection of the authentic, just as you would expect of rituals that have been pasturized for public consumption.

Essential to the understanding of Kahuna magic is that they saw each human being as having three souls or spirits that resided within. These three souls, or spirits, the Kahunas called the *Unihipili*, the *Uhane*, and the *Aumakau*. It is the roots that are contained in the very words that gave Max Freedom Long his first clues to breaking the secret system of Kahuna magic.

The *Unihipili* correlates to the subconscious in modern psychology. The *Uhane* and the *Unihipili* are two separate spirits that inhabit one body. The two spirits work as a team. Each has functions that rely on the abilities of the other, and each needs the physical medium of the human body.

The *Aumakua* translates literally as the older, parental, clearly trustworthy pair—meaning that it is composed of a male and female essence, a balance and a polarity that is necessary for working any magical system on the earth plane. This dual spirit has both the lower self, the *Unihipili*, and the middle self, *Uhane*, under its guidance and protection. It occupies the level of consciousness immediately above our own conscious level, and it corresponds to the superconscious in psychology.

The *Aumakua*, called the high self, is the highest god with whom the Kahunas ever dealt. They believed in the supreme creative force, but they did not believe that they could pray to it or appease it. The only level of consciousness that they felt they could humanly comprehend was the one in which they were dwelling. Their only contact with a level directly above their own was due to their connection with the high self, the *Aumakua*.

The other essential element in understanding Kahuna magic is that of the *Aka* substance. According to Kahuna belief, surrounding these three spirits—or selves—within each human are three invisible or shadowy bodies. These shadowy selves correspond to the etheric and the astral doubles of occult literature. These amorphous bodies are made up of what the Kahunas called the *Aka*.

The *Aka* substance formed the sheath or a cloak in which the three souls of man could reside. There was one sheath for each respective soul, with varying degrees of intensity. The *Aka* could also be likened in spiritualist belief structure to ectoplasm, and it plays a central role in such things as telepathy and psychology.

The *Aka* substance is said to be sticky in Kahuna magic, thereby explaining how one can touch an object and symbolically connect himself to the *Aka* thread that is still bound in the spirit substance to the person who has owned that object before. The spirit self within the medium travels the *Aka* thread to gain information about the previous owner of the watch or the ring, whatever object he may be holding.

Another essential item in understanding Kahuna is that of the *Mana*. The *Mana* is a vital force which reposes in the human body. It is the low self which produces simple *Mana*. The middle self uses the *Mana-mana*, Mana with a higher voltage so to speak. The high self uses *Mana-loa*. The electromagnetic voltage used by the high self is so supercharged that it has extraordinary properties, literally able to smash atoms of reality.

As we learn more about our world, we see that all is energy, all is vibration, and all is one form or another of a manifestation of the electromagnetic spectrum.

Max Freedom Long, in his early research, presumed that these voltages were electrical. Low *Mana* could be likened to the body waves, which have been recorded scientifically in the laboratory. *Mana-mana* may correspond to the brain waves, and *Mana-loa* could find its counterpart in the *Chi*, the *Ki*, the *Holy Spirit*, the *Wakan-tonka*—that vital substance that inhabits and moves through every living thing and can be focused by the human psyche literally to create miracles.

The most essential element necessary for success in Kahuna magic is contact with a high self. It is on this level above our own conscious level that the power is sufficient to perform physical miracles. The Huna thought contact with the superconscious could only be made by the low self acting under orders from the middle self. The low self is connected to the high self by a shadowy cord, the *Aka*, made of the same substance as the shadowy bodies. When contact is desired, it is achieved by the flow of *Mana* up the *Aka* until the high self is reached.

Now, unfortunately, especially for beginners, it is not unusual for some sort of blockage to appear, making contact very difficult. The blockage, unless it is caused by the intervention of the external spirit, usually occurs on the subconscious level.

The low self, it was believed by the Kahunas, served as the seat of memory, in which all the thought forms that have been created by the middle self are stored. You must remember also that, in the Kahuna system, thoughts really *are* things. Each thought literally becomes a tiny bead of *Aka* substance which clusters around the other thoughts of a similar nature.

When you require a specific piece of information, your middle self simply instructs your low self to produce the necessary information. The whole cluster of *Aka* beads are reviewed, explaining in Kahuna terms why memory is associational.

The low self is the creator of emotions. Within it are formed such emotional responses as fear and guilt and pride.

It is guilt, however, and all those emotions that are associated with it, that most concerns us as spiritual alchemists, for those are the emotions which can inhibit contact with the high self. If the low self does something of which it is ashamed, it will try to avoid the high self, much as the

The Hawaiians, who followed the general pattern of religion which their ancestors brought from central Polynesia, had many gods who rendered help in the needs and activities of this life. The gods, though regarded as invisible spirits, were symbolized by material objects, some of natural wood or stone and others made in the image of man, in part or in whole. Supernatural help was obtained by reciting an appropriate formula and accompanying it with some offering laid before the symbol or altar of the god.   Bishop Museum

naughty child stricken with remorse or fear of punishment will seek to avoid its parents.

Guilt and fear can become fixed thought forms in the low self. Every time the middle self instructs the low self to contact the high self, it can collide with those emotions and be unable to make contact. We see, then, in terms of the Kahuna cosmology, why the individual may often find himself at the mercy of his unreasonable subconscious self.

In our modern society an individual faced with such a problem will go to a psychoanalyst. In Hawaii years ago (and in some cases *today*—if one knows where to acquire a Kahuna priest) one would go to a Kahuna to solve such a problem.

Of special use to students of magic is the utilization of the great *Ha* prayer rite. It was the correct use of the *Ha* prayer rite that enabled ancient Kahunas to contact that intangible energy (the X-force, the Unknown Energy) that answers prayers—and from the human perspective, literally performs miracles.

It is necessary to be able to reach the high self to perform any type of magic, and this rite can be used by anyone who earnestly desires to establish that type of contact. If you correctly follow this format and practice it, you will be able to accomplish the same kind of feats of telepathy, clairvoyance, and healing that the Kahunas did regularly in earlier times—and still do in secret today.

Basically, you must instruct the conscious or the middle self to be able to approach the high self. It cannot of itself do that. Only the subconscious can reach the high self. The role of the conscious self is to instruct the low self to accumulate an extra supply of *mana,* which is to be held in readiness.

The subconscious, acting under the orders of the middle self, is to reach up the connecting *Aka* cord and make contact with the high self. It is the high self, once this contact has been made, that will bring about the desired wishes expressed in the prayer. The prayer can be brought about only by the integrated efforts of the three composite selves.

There are four basic steps in the *Ha* prayer rite; but before mentioning them, two additional elements must be stressed. These are consistency and repetition. It is important that the high self receives a clear and unwavering picture of the situation or the object that you desire through your prayer. If the high self picks up the contradictions and fragments of a constantly changing image, it will be confused, or the power of the prayer will be greatly diminished. The correct image must be constantly fed to the high self, and it is the proper practice of this rite that will guarantee that the proper energy is directed in the proper way.

In order to keep the image as clear as possible, you should carefully choose the prayer that you wish to make. You should know in advance which image you intend to send to your higher self. If you have done the work of deciding these things before the actual work of your prayerful undertaking, you should not have to worry about sending a confused request.

Here are the four basic steps in performing the Ha prayer rite:

First, the middle self will instruct the low self to create an extra amount of *Mana*. This is done by taking four deep breaths. These breaths should be taken in very slowly, and the breathing should be practiced very much like the deep breathing exercises of the Yogis. Once the *Mana* or the vital force has been aroused, it is held in readiness.

With the accumulated *Mana* still residing in the lower self, the subconscious reaches up along the shadowy *Aka* cord until the high self has been successfully contacted.

When this contact is assured, the low self releases its store of *Mana* in a kind of sacrificial gift to the high self. The high self will use its vital force to formulate the answer to the prayer.

Finally, rising up the *Aka* cord with the *Mana* is the mental image of the thing desired by you.

The repetition of this rite is so necessary that it should be considered a fifth step. And not only should the clear picture be continually projected, but so should the daily supply of *Mana*. *Mana* strengthens the high self. Without *Mana* the high self would be too weak to accomplish anything in the physical world in which we live.

Another way to accumulate an excessive amount of *Mana* in the lower self is to stand in the star position; that is, feet wide apart, arms extending at the sides, level with the shoulders. Next, repeat the affirmation, "The universal light force is flowing through me now. I feel it!"

If you were to add the four deep breaths of Huna to this exercise, a considerable supply of *Mana* could be realized for use by the high self.

The initial formulation of the prayer is essential to the success of the *Ha* rite. The attitude one develops pertaining to the prayer is also of vital importance.

We have been told in innumerable sources that "whatsoever things you desire, believe that you have them, and you shall have them." The element of belief is of great importance for the successful application of the *Ha* prayer.

Throughout the actual rite, the individual must rest in a quiet faith that the high self is already taking care of the request. Just as one can plant a seed and see it grow into a plant and pick the fruit, so should one envision the path taken by one specific prayer. The seed must eventually be trusted to bear fruit. The length of time involved simply depends on the nature of the request. Some changes, of course, will require considerably more time than others.

In addition to a lack of belief, two other factors might interfere with the success of the prayer rite—mainly guilt and spirit intervention. A sense of guilt imbedded in the subconscious would inhibit contact with the high self. The high self is always willing to give aid to the two lower selves; but if the subconscious does not feel worthy of any assistance, it would be afraid to approach the high self. Sometimes this situation can result from an actual sense of wrong doing. But, more often it is like the child who desires punishment for his real or imagined sins.

Spirit intervention is difficult to explain to some people who are locked totally into what they consider to be the modern world. However, integral to an understanding of both American Indian magic and Kahuna magic is a total belief in a partnership with the world of spirits.

In order for a prayer to be successful, you must look to the request and to the motivation. The Kahunas were emphatic in their belief that the high self. the utterly trustworthy, parental pair, could perform no ill to anyone. The two lower selves, regrettably, did have this failing. But if they ever chose to harm someone, it was an action divorces from the high self. The *Ha* prayer rite cannot be successfully employed if you seek to harm (either physically or emotionally) another.

The Ha prayer rite works because the high self has the ability to change the future. This is what prayer is all about. If you wish to change an annoying condition, it is because you are convinced that certain undesirable factors show no signs of changing themselves, but will continue a negative course into the future.

The high self builds the future for you, using your mental images as its tools. That is why the proper formulation of goals is so important. Obviously, if a consistent image is projected, a consistent future will be constructed.

If the only tools the high self has to work with are a jumble of chaotic impressions. the pattern it creates will show a corresponding confusion. Once you employ this knowledge of the future-changing ability of the high self, you will carefully choose the correct prayer, and faithfully repeat it every day.

As I said, the Kahunas believed that thoughts were things, that they were composed of the same *Aka* substance as the three shadowy bodies. Each time you formulate the *Ha* prayer it comes a microscopic bead on the *Aka* thread. For each repetition a duplicate bead is made, and the stronger becomes the strand. The Kahuna system may actually explain the mechanics of the positive thinking approach, which teaches one constantly to project a positive mental attitude.

In Kahuna theory, if you should desire to make telepathic contact with another, your subconscious self must first cast out a thread of the *Aka,* or shadowy body stuff, to connect itself to the subconscious of the person with whom communion is desired. It is the Kahuna belief that the subconscious has the strange and marvelous ability to project a portion of its shadowy body in much the same manner as an amoeba projects a part of its body in which to make a "hand" with which to grasp a particle of food. In telepathy or mind reading, the Kahuna practitioner will first visualize or project a "hand" being formed and extended toward the person it wishes to contact. Upon reaching the subject, it becomes necessary to pierce and to enter the shadowy body of the person, just as a spear would pierce the physical body.

You must remember that, according to Kahuna theory the subject, if aware of an effort to touch and to pierce through his invisible body, could usually cause his subconscious to repel such an approach. This could be accomplished through an effort of the will of the subject's middle self or conscious mind.

Once contact has been made with a subject who does not resist, a thread of shadowy stuff connects the two individuals. Along this thread travels a flow of the low *mana* of the vital force. When you have become connected in this way with your subject, you have become joined with him or her through an electrically charged invisible cord.

Your subconscious may project a tiny part of its sensory organs to the far end of the cord and observe what thoughts are passing through the mind of your subject. Your subconscious is less able to duplicate these thoughts as thought forms in their individual shadowy bodies and send them back in the flow of vital force to your center of consciousness.

Once this has been accomplished, thoughts of your subject are presented to the focus of consciousness of your middle self, much as the memory is presented by the low self in desires and they become known to you.

The first and most important thing to remember in the *Huna* system is to understand that the low self has in its shadowy body duplicates of every cell and tissue of the physical body, thus duplicating all sensory organs.

Astral travel in the *Huna* system is dependent upon how much of the low shadowy body you choose to project. If only a small part is projected, a center of consciousness remains in the physical body, which contains the mass of the low shadowy body. If the mass of the low shadowy body is projected leaving only a thickish thread of shadowy substance to connect with the physical body (astral cord) the center of consciousness necessarily moves with the greater part of the shadowy body and becomes actually present at the distant place which is visited.

The Kahunas believe that the great events of the future were set and can be foreseen far ahead. World or national events might be seen hundreds or even thousands of years ahead. The future of the individual, because of the shortness of the human life span, could be seen only months or years ahead.

The Kahunas often demonstrated their abilities to change the future for the individual, for their most essential belief was that the future was not irrevocable. The future could be changed, they believed; and frequently, it seems they did so.

According to Huna, it is the high self that constructs the future out of the thoughts and imagination of the middle self. This jumble of conflicting desires and fears is related to the high self then takes those thoughts formed of *Aka* substance and fastens it to a very real future. Just as the physical body sets the mold of high self's shadowy body, so do events and people fit this future mold created by the high self.

Sleep is the most common time for thought forms to travel up the *Aka* cord to the high self. For in sleep, conscious barriers are lowered and the suggestible sleep consciousness is more easily reached. Anyone desiring to influence actively the thought forms chosen by the high self to used in forming the future should begin his work with the sleep state. The subconscious self is extremely impressionable. It is also incapable of any other than very rudimentary powers of reasoning. If a thought can be lodged in it, the subconscious would be persuaded to hand the thought form over to the high self.

In planning for the future, thoughts lodged in the low self would be the ones used by the high self to build a corresponding future. One method of influencing the future is to imply thought forms in the low self when it is asleep—its most suggestible period. This can be done with tape recorders set to play the desired message to the low self. When the tape recorder is used on a regular basis, the individual will adjust to the disturbance and cease to wake up when the message is played. The advantage of this method is that the message is being relayed to the low self at the time when contact with the high self is most propitious.

When a Kahuna prayed to his or her self asking aid for a client, the prayer automatically went to the high self of the client as well. This involved the belief that all high selves were linked together in some way. The high selves are many in one, one in many. They are unity and separation. They have bonds closer that those of bees in a hive. They have learned to work as a unit, but each does individual works.

The Kahunas had a very simple way of determining what was sin and what was not. One asked oneself if any act was such that it injured another or hurt another's feelings. If the act hurt no one in any way, it was not considered a sin.

The Kahuna system taught that God was too high and too powerful for any human being to be hurt by any mortal act. Again and again, a Kahuna might answer an orthodox Christian missionary, "I cannot sin against God: I am too small."

Before a healing can ever be accomplished, the Kahunas believe, there must be no sense of doubt or a conviction of sin or a guilt that has not been cleared away. That which we might call "faith," they would consider a condition of mental freedom from any hindering complex.

One Kahuna referred to a complex or a fixation of ideas as "the thing eating inside." A conviction held by the low self may not be a correct belief, but once it is fixed in the memory of the low self, it is difficult to find—and even more difficult to remove.

The Kahuna theory of instant healing is one which involves (1) a high self with a superior form of mentality and an ability to do the work: (2) the high voltage of vital force or *mana*, natural to all high selves and used in all miraculous works; and (3) the flesh, bone, and blood of the injured limb, and the Aka or shadowy body of the patient—particularly that part of it which duplicates the injured part of the body.

The Kahunas believe that this shadowy body of the low self is a mold of every cell of the body, also of its general shape. To heal a broken bone, the high self dissolves the injured bone and injured tissues into ectoplasm. The shadowy body mold is made of an invisible substance that cannot be broken or injured. Thus with the mold of the normal leg there at hand, the ectoplasmic material of the dissolved parts is resolidified in the mold with the result that the healing is instant, and the limb is restored to its former condition. If there would be a physical or a degenerative disease, such as cancer, it would be changed to an ectoplasmic substance and then made into normal tissue to form the mold of that part of the body, as it was before the cancer developed.

The basic method of staying in good health would be always to send carefully the proper pictures of your desired state of health to your high self. You must picture yourself in perfect health and impress that image on the low self as a thing to send as a desire to your high self. In this manner, the low self would create a picture of you in perfect health and project the image upward. The way the high self answers this prayer is to materialize the picture into reality for you.

Understand though, that the picture of yourself in perfect health must **not** include your illness. Too often you may pray, "Oh, please, God, heal my sickness." And, with such a prayer, goes the picture from the low self of you in a sick and miserable condition. At the same time, the low self might also squeeze in a fuzzy picture of you as well and healthy. But the result would be confusion, and nothing will cause the high self to change your confusion.

You must **believe** that you are receiving perfect health. You must hold the thought of yourself as well and happy. Make and memorize the picture of you in good health, then conduct proper breathing exercises in order to conduct the *Mana* and to give the picture enough strength to hold together while the high self materializes it into actuality for you.

After that you should instruct your low self to send the picture and a large amount of *Mana* to the high self, like a telepathic message. Repeat the prayer action at least once a day, and continue until the desire results are achieved. Tell yourself that perfect health is already given to the high self. It is already real. **Live** in the picture. **Feel** it. Keep your mind off your illness. This is the key to your magic. It is yours to use if you will.

Here are the ten basic elements in Kahuna magic:

1. There are three spirits that compose the human being, whether the person is living or deceased. There are (A) the subconscious, which remembers, but has defective reason. It creates all emotions. (B) The conscious, which remembers, but has full reasoning power. (C) The superconscious, which has a process of realizing. It knows the past, the present, and as much of the future as has been crystalized or definitely planned, created, or projected on its level.

2. There are three voltages of vital force *(Mana)* which are used by the three spirits of humankind.

A. The body waves, or low-voltage, vital electrical force. It is used by the subconscious and can flow over threads of shadowy body substance—the *Aka*. It can carry chemical substance with it as it flows from person to person. It can take the force of magnetism and be stored in wood and other porous substances. A large discharge of this low-voltage vital force commanded by the will can exert a paralyzing effect or a hypnotic effect, resulting in unconsciousness, sleep, and the rigid or cataleptic state.

B. The brain waves or vital force of the next higher voltage is used by the conscious mind spirit in all it thinking and willing activities. Used at will, it can be a hypnotic force, provided that a thought form is introduced into the mind of the subject. It cannot travel over the shadowy substance threads, as can the lower voltage.

C. The high voltage or vital fore that is thought by the Kahunas to be used by the superconscious for its various purposes correlates to that energy which I have termed the X-force.

3. There are invisible or shadowy substance bodies in which the three spirits which compose humankind reside. The lower two usually interblend with each other and with the body during life. They remain interblended after death unless separated by some unfortunate circumstances.

A. The shadowy body of the subconscious is the most dense of the three. It is of such a nature that it sticks to whatever we touch, or perhaps even that which we see or hear. And when removed for the contact it draws out a long visible thread of itself, which connects the person with the thing contacted in a form of semipermanent union. All things were supposed by the Kahunas to have a shadowy body, be they crystals, plants, animals, fabricated articles, humans. This substance is an ideal conductor of vital electrical force or currents, and can be used as a strong place for it. When heavily charged with the low voltage of the force, it becomes rigid and firm enough to be used as a "hand" or an instrument to move or affect physical objects.

B. The shadowy substance of the conscious mind—spirit or humankind is less dense than that of the subconscious. It seems not to be sticky or to pull out into threads. It may or may not be a conductor of low voltage vital force, but undoubtedly is a conductor of the middle voltage—its own peculiar voltage as used in its form of mental activity and will. It forms the ghostly body in which the spirit functions as a spirit after death.

C. The shadowy body of the superconscious spirit resides in this invisible and very light body at all times, seldom making direct contact with the physical body by entering it. By analogy, it is supposed to have characteristics somewhat resembling the shadowy bodies of the two lower spirits.

Though buffalo and other wild animals can be seen in these and other Indian "rock writings", according to Hopi historian White Bear, these petroglyphs also show what look like jet aircraft and flying saucers leading some researchers to believe that the Hopi "came from out there."

7.

CHAPTER THIRTEEN

Do The Hopis Hold the Key to Amerindian Magic?

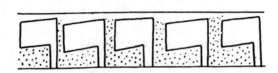

Carved on a rock near the village of Oraibi, Arizona, in the heart of Hopi land, is a petroglyphic representation that records the prophecy of the Great Spirit in regard to His return.

In the lower left-hand corner are a bow and an arrow, representing the material tools which the Great Spirit, who stands to the right of the implements, gave to the Hopi.

The Great Spirit points to his path, which is straight up. An upper path to the Great Spirit's right is the white man's way. Two white men and one Hopi—symbolizing the Hopi who forsake the old traditions and adopt other ways—walk this line. A vertical line joins the path of the white man with that of the Hopi, indicating their contact since the Hopi's emergence from the Lower World. The Hopi's path is lower, more spiritual, than the way of the white man.

A large circle represents World War I, another stands for World War II. A third circle symbolizes the Great Purification, which the Hopi feel is fast approaching, according to a timetable that was set centuries ago.

After this transitional period, the Great Spirit returns; food and water is abundant; the world is made well. The white man's path becomes more and more erratic until it is but a series of dots that eventually fade away.

A quartered circle in the lower right hand corner of the petroglyph is the familiar symbol for the spiritual center of the North American continent, which the Hopi believe is the Southwestern United States, specifically the area around Oraibi.

"At one time I thought my people, the Cherokee, held the answer," Don Wilkerson said to me, "but now I tend to believe that the Hopis hold the secret. A lot of this is touchy ground. Much of it is conjecture, but the Hopis have done things that are unbelievable."

In the Hopi myths of their people emerging from one world to another, we may have a poetic accounting of a people's intellectual and spiritual evolution, or we may have exactly what the traditional Hopis claim: the record of major high civilizations that rose and collapsed in prehistorical times. One may call these civilizations Mu, Lemuria, Atlantis, it matters little; but the Hopis myths maintain that that human race has passed through three worlds which the Great Spirit has been forced to terminate, to purify, because of the people's corruption and materialism.

The last Great Destruction was achieved by flood, and all but a few faithful perished. The story of the Great Deluge has survived in the myths of nearly every culture, and it is said that the Hopi and all those faithful who

127

were saved made a covenant with the Great Spirit that they would never again turn away from His path. But now, the Hopi believe, the Fourth World is coming to a close. Men had fallen away from their covenant with the Great Spirit. Once again, a Great Purification is needed.

The Hopis believe that the Great Spirit did interact with the first people and that He taught them how to live and how to worship. He breathed His teachings, prophecies, and warnings on stone tablets, before He hid Himself from the view of man. Spider Woman and her two grandsons, the Great Spirit's helpers, remained, along with other guiding spirits. These tablets were broken in half by the spirit Massau when the Hopis reached this continent. Today the traditional Hopis await the return of the Older Brother, whose skin has since turned white, who will match his share of the sacred stone tablets with those retained by his Younger Brother. The rejoining of the sacred tablets will signal the advent of Purification Day.

The Hopis were led to their present home in Arizona by a star. As Abraham dealt with his nephew Lot, the Hopis chose desolate and infertile land and permitted other tribes to choose the greener, more fertile valleys. Or so it may seem to those with greedy eyes. The Hopis settled here because it is the land of the Great Spirit. In spite of the sparse quality of their home, the Hopis were warned, strangers would come and try to take it away from them. The Hopis must resist all pressures, they were told, and they must hold on to the land and their ancient religion. If they were able to retain control of their material and spiritual gifts of the Great Spirit and remain true to their name ("one who follow the peaceful path"), Hopi land would one day be the spiritual center from which all Indians would be reawakened to the old traditions and would arise to touch the hearts and save the souls of the invading strangers.

"There are shrines there in the spiritual center which are markers for spiritual routes which extend in all four directions to the edge of the continent," *Clear Creek* magazine quoted an elderly traditional Hopi. "Through our ceremonies it is possible to keep the natural forces together. From here at the spiritual center, our prayer go to all parts of the Earth. Our prayers are the balance that keep all things well and healthy. This is the sacred place. It must never be defiled ... Only people who know how to grow things will survive. Through prayer, people can develop their own way, as the Hopi have."

(That same issue of *Clear Creek, The Environmental Viewpoint*, No. 13, is largely devoted to the crisis at Black Mesa, wherein coal is being strip-mined for a consortium of twenty-three power companies (Western Energy Supply and Transmission Association). According to Ms. Melissa Savage: "This land of wide, silent deserts and deep sky-space will soon contain six giant power plants which will make up the heart of the energy grid ... Together all six plants will be able to generate some 14,000 megawatts (MW), yet this is just the beginning. By 1985, the WEST consortium plans to operate plants with a generating capacity of 36,000 MW, 17 times the capacity of Egypt's famed Aswan Dam." Since Black Mesa is considered by the Hopi to be the spiritual center of this continent, one can imagine the horror the uninformed traditionalists experienced when they learned of the planned desecration. Mrs. Mina Lansa told the United States Senate: "We are holding the land for the Great Spirit ... We heard about the Black Mesa coal mine.The land is ours and Black Mesa is on the shrine that belongs to (Hopi chiefs) and the Spirit gave it to us. We heard that the Hopi Tribal Council members and the Navajo Council members, too, are the ones leasing to the Peabody (Mining Company). We are very sorry that they never asked permission of us. ...I am very worried for my people. I don't want them to starve ... I am like the mother of the earth because I am holding the land. We ... hold the whole world all over. I am worrying about it all the time ..." *How long will we permit commercial interests to upset our continent's spiritual, as well as ecological balance?*)

The Hopi traditionalist refer to their prophecies and agree that the Older Brother will soon return with his half of the Sacred Tablets. The prophecies state that the Great Purification will occur when people turn to material, rather that spiritual, things; when evil ones set out to destroy the land and the life of the Hopi and other Indian brothers; when leaders of men turn to evil instead of the Great Spirit; when man has invented something which can fall upon the ground, boil everything within a great area, and turn the land to ashes where no grass will grow. It would seem that each of these specifications has been fulfilled.

The Hopis are not alone in their anticipation of a Great Purification. Don Wanatee says the Mesquakie, a people who have proudly maintained the old traditions, see a great catastrophe happening soon to "rearrange things":

It will possibly be a great fire of some type, and it will leave pockets of men and women who will begin to people the Earth again. This is what the prophets of the Mesquakie have maintained. They have prophesied that the

130 many people with their many languages will want to come back to their old religion. These people will want to return to the traditionalists to learn. There are traditional pockets in Mexico and in the United States. People here in Iowa have called us heathens, pagans. We shall see we are all brothers after all.

I think the end might be very near. I am not speaking as a pessimist, but as one who believes in the prophecies of the Mesquakie. A hundred years ago, the Mesquakie prophesied a box that would sit in the corner in which we would see things happening far away and hear people speaking who would not be there. They prophesied great trailways in the sky. They said that the animals would be dying. They said when many species were becoming extinct, man would begin to see unusual things. Floods, earthquakes. It would be as if the Earth were revolting against its inhumane treatment.

Other Indian tribes throughout the country are beginning to see these things coming. Many are saying in desperation, "What can we do to revive the old tradition? How can we get back to it?" Well, there is a way for them to return, of course; but time is very short. They had better start returning now, or else they are going to be left on the railway station when the train leaves. You know, it is all going to be over.

Hopi traditionalists are storing food and water for the coming Great Purification. They have been told that there will be a terrible famine sometime soon—no longer than two or three years in the future. Canned and dehydrated foods, seed, kerosene lamps, bottled water and water purification tablets are being put aside in carefully concealed caches.

The Chicago medium Deon Frey related an interesting experience which she shared with a delegation of Hopi who were traveling to Washington and the United Nations to declare a warning of the coming Time of Purification:

We went to what they called a Council of Mankind. It was held in the city of Chicago at the university. There were spiritual leaders representing each country in the world. This meeting was unknown to me. I had seen nothing on television, not had I heard anything about it on radio, or read about it in the newspaper. Someone said the W. Clement Stone, the insurance man, had paid large sums of money to keep it going.

The odd part of it was that we had to be known by someone in attendance before we could be admitted. Without my even knowing I would attend—one of the Hopis, who said he was 103 years old, had invited me—I was ushered in what seemed like separate boxes arranged in a circle. Each representative from these individual countries was to stand and give his view of what he thought the world was coming to and what could be done to save mankind and what we could do to help the people understand what is happening. Each representative wore his own dress and stated views of his own faith.

We were not allowed outside of the building once the sessions had begun. Lunch was served there and everything was free. After breaks, we would return to the sessions and the individuals statements would resume. We were there in session for three days. The Hopis told us about the Older White Brother and the secret of what was to happen in our world.

When the meetings were over, I accompanied the Hopis to a place where they told us more things and said how they would meditate and receive these things directly from Spirit. At that time they already had three years of food stored away. One of the men claimed to have half of the original stone which would fit with the White Brother's other half.

The elderly man explained to me how they traveled at night, by what I would call astral travel. The Hopis visualize themselves in a boat moving on a stream. He said that if I ever wanted to get in touch with them, I should visualize myself in a boat coming toward them, and they would be able to pick me up.

I have tried this and it has worked. I have visualized the blue water, the canoe, and myself in the canoe paddling toward them. The Hopi seem to be able to pick up that vibration quite easily. This seems to be one of their ways of attuning themselves to the white man.

I was given a spiritual name by the Hopis, a name which meant something to them and to me. I was honored that they considered me spiritual enough to accept their ideas and to understand them. Very often we could just look at each other and tell what the other was thinking. We did not always have to use words to communicate. The Hopis are very aware.

The Hopis told about the Great Purification that is coming sooner than we think. This is why they store up food. There will be a great catastrophe, and they believe that their home in the Southwest is the safest place to be.

When non-Indian Paul Solem told the media that he had been sent to the Hopi reservation to "call down" UFOs to present the Hopis with a sign, then produced what the waiting, skeptical press called "a flying saucer" ("It looked like a star—almost. It rose in the sky, stopped, hovered, wavered to one side and then continued across the sky repeating the maneuvers" [Joe Kraus, Managing Editor, Prescott *Courier,* August 9, 1970]), he provoked yet another split among the traditional Hopi. But 109-year-old Chief Dan Katchongva said that both the division and the UFOs are in fulfillment of the old prophecies foretelling the Great Purification:

"A petroglyph near Mishongnovi on Second Mesa shows flying saucers and travel through space. The arrow on which the dome-shaped object rests, stands for travel through space. the Hopi maiden on the dome shape represents purity. Those Hopi who survive Purification Day will be taken to other planets. We, the faithful Hopi, have seen the ships and know they are true. We have watched nearly all our brethren lose faith in the original teachings and go off on their own course. Near Oraibi was closely shown the Plan of Life, and we are gathered here to await our True White Brother."

Paul Solem claims that the UFOs are piloted by a people descended from the Ten Lost Tribes of Israel. The Hopi share this lineage, and the Great Star which led them to Oraibi was a guiding UFO. Certain Hopis state that the ships are manned by Kachinas, entities which are portrayed in traditional Hopi dances.

"I doubt very much if you will find another Indian who will tell you this," I was told by an Amerindian who has made a study of the origins of his people, "but I don't believe that there is any doubt whatsoever that there are Indian people on the face of this Earth who did not originate on this planet. I tend to think that once the Hopi prophecies are carried out and their revelations are made know, they will bear this out. The Hopis came from *out there*."

"Many people have said that our picture-craft is nothing but primitive doodling," White Bear, a Hopi historian and traditionalist remarked, "but centuries and centuries ago, the Hopi drew a jet airplane on a rock which depicted our people arriving from the birthplace of our fathers. Yes, centuries ago, we had a picturecraft of a flying saucer."

White Bear provided the drawings and source material for the classic Frank Waters volume *The Book of the Hopi.* Since I am honored to count White Bear and his charming wife Naomi as friends, I have the privilege of including an interview with White Bear in this book.

Do you agree with me that the power , richness, and relevance of Amerindian magic are being reborn in our decade?

White Bear: That is a positive truth. As far as our side of knowledge is concerned, this is due to the planetary system which is forcing man to come to full realization and to see that this may be obtained from our tribal religious order.

There are certain events that are taking place now which we know give evidence that the old traditions are regaining strength. These activities are going on in the atmosphere, as well as in human affairs. This is why, as a Hopi, I am very concerned that people are coming to full realization now.

What special insights might you, as a wise man of your people, share that will help us all come to full realization?

White Bear: As far as the events that are occurring in our nation today, this is an important part of our prophecies. There is so much evidence here (Oraibi) that I can give, but I am concerned how many people will get to realize it and acknowledge it. In the first place, I will have to get rid of my skin before everyone will accept my knowledge. Prejudice is a great barrier.

Skin color offers no barriers between brothers of the soul; but, unfortunately, for some, pigmentation does present a problem.

White Bear: Well, that has been the greatest opposition to the white people accepting our knowledge and recognizing what we can bring to them. My uncle made a trip to Washington back in 1890 and tried to warn the government about the events in time that would take place.

You feel that a message of great importance has been presented to contemporary man in your ancient Hopi prophecies, but that this message has been continually ignored.

White Bear: Exactly. But who are we? We are not an aggressive people. We are not going to make any kind of aggressive movement against someone who is doing wrong to us. We leave all things to our Divine Creator to straighten up.

We see now more Amerindians reviving interest in their native traditions and in their native religious philosophies.

White Bear: Yes, but you see two types of Indian movements. There are two types of forces that are now active. One is the aggressive, and the

133

other is a spiritual movement. The spiritual movement will prevail and become stronger, because the aggressive force will get caught up in national affairs and lose sight of important issues.

What is your opinion of the use of psychotropic drugs as an aid to spiritual development?

White Bear: To tell you the truth, for those who truly wish to advance in spiritual ways, to resort to marijuana, peyote, and these other things is wrong. Completely wrong. I cannot go along with these things. My people cannot.

You are saying that there are no shortcuts to true spirituality?

White Bear: That is right. You have to start from within. You cannot receive your upliftment from chemicals. Meditate. Receive important messages from your dreams.

Do you feel that the religious traditions of Europe and Asia—Christianity, Buddhism, Judaism, etc.—may be compatible with your ancient traditions?

White Bear: According to that part of the prophecy, there will be a spiritual awakening in the continents you mention, but they must come to America. This is where the freedom was. This is where the true spirit of the Brotherhood was established. Regardless of how many religious orders they may have set up thousands of years ago, we are the people who have not contaminated the true spiritual knowledge.

White Bear, can you speak frankly about our future survival as a species?

White Bear: If you want me to say that we are going to clean up this mess that has been made, I cannot. The pollution of our atmosphere is the worst thing that man has done. This pollution will get into our soil and into the physical parts of our people, as a whole race of mankind. Worse, not only will people's bodies be contaminated, but their spirits. The Hopi are trying their best to awaken all the nations of the world to this part of our prophecy.

Do you see any particular areas that will be healthier after the Great Purification?

White Bear: As far as our knowledge is concerned, the area within one hundred miles of Oraibi is the best. Scientists have found no evidence of contamination of our soil. There is no radioactive fallout. That is why we are here. That is why we came here centuries ago. We had full knowledge of this before we came.

What is so mystical about that area around Oraibi?

White Bear: If you had been here with us and with our guests from Europe, from India, from Japan, from Korea, you would have felt this strong feeling. (White Bear was mildly put out with me at the time of this interview, because I had been unable to witness a special ceremony due to a personal complication which prevented me from being in attendance.)

When do you look for the return of the Older White Brother?

White Bear: Some people think, you know, that this refers to the modern white man, but this is not so. We refer to the spiritual brother who has understanding of all kinds. He is not of human flesh at the moment, but he will come. Certain aggressive actions by nations, who call themselves the Great Powers, will set in motion a certain event that will lead to the coming of the True White Brother.

Do you see this happening before the end of our century?

White Bear: Not quite. All has been arranged. There is nothing new. There has been a great program laid out. Everybody has to go by the schedule of the weeks. The weeks run from Sunday to Sunday. There are certain things that people may do in between, but they must arrive at the next Sunday. There are things on the great program that may take years and years to fulfilled, but all things are laid down on the schedule.

And everything is going according to schedule?

White Bear: That is right. In fact, we are now delaying the schedule by fifteen years.

The schedule is now fifteen years behind?

White Bear: That is right. I wish you would have been here to witness the ceremonies, and you would have known exactly what is going on.

What do you think is happening now with non-Indian youth who are seeking to emulate the Indian lifestyle and religious philosophy?

White Bear: There are great universal powers which are making young people got into these activities without their having full knowledge. Unfortunately, not all of these young people are motivated by spiritual things, and they are destructive.

Can their energies be made constructive, rather than destructive?

135

White Bear: I wish it could be that way, As far as their adopting our tribal ways and customs, we are trying to keep ourselves clean. The opposite force is being used among these young people. It is the wrong kind.

What guidance can you give young people to make their lives more positive?

White Bear: Many of these young people come from wonderful people, but until they learn the true way of getting on the right course of the spiritual life through meditation, this opposite force will continue to motivate them. Some speak of having lived before as Hopis. I am positive this is not so. They are more aggressive in their way of conduct than I would be if I were being reborn again.

So when young people come to you, you look at their spiritual attitude; and you find that it is more aggressive than it should be.

White Bear: That is right. When you deal with the human action on the opposite side, well, then you know their spiritual attitude just isn't right. They are too rebellious. But I am trying my best to do what I can to try to help our nation's young people.

We Hopis have our doctrine and complete, full knowledge in our sacred tablets. You know that Naomi and I are going to present this evidence in our new book that we are working on. What we have can offer true spiritual guidance for modern man. This has to be brought out in the type of work that you are doing. We Hopis are the only people who have this knowledge within our souls. We have kept ourselves uncontaminated.

If the Hopis hold the secret of Amerindian mysticism, then it is a secret that has to do with the Amerindians'—and perhaps all peoples'—true place of origin and the true nature of man's spiritual inheritance. The Hopis claim that humankind has been engaged in its struggle for spiritual perfection for aeons longer than our orthodox science can either conceive or acknowledge. If the Hopis' tablets record more than a symbolic representation of man's social, intellectual, and metaphysical evolution and do actually carry an account of the progression of sophisticated civilizations that have risen and fallen as the victims of their own materialistic technologies, then the Hopi prophecies indicate a time spiral, a calendar of time, that warns us that our own days are numbered and that a Great Purification is overdue. Now, more than ever before, humankind needs to walk in balance and become receptive channels to the Great Spirit.

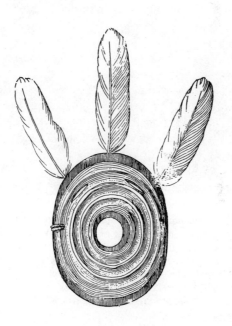

Twylah Nitsch, the granddaughter of Moses Shongo, the last great Seneca
Medicine Man, continues the tradition of her family by passing down her
wisdom to the youngest member of the tribe.
To the American Indian, the young are of tremendous importance,
for it is they who will see the great prophecies of their
forefathers come to pass.
(photo credit: Robert Koch)

CHAPTER FOURTEEN

The Seven Worlds

Has civilization on Earth been cyclical? Have there been highly evolved human or hominid cultures before the tradition that led to our epoch? Do memories of glorious time before our own lie half forgotten within man's collective unconscious? Have entire civilizations attained the apex of cultural accomplishment to be crushed during their very golden day to become, a few thousand years later, little more than rumors and twice-told tales. Have mighty empires risen to wax strong and conquer the Earth, only to have their vibrant flames snuffed out in global catastrophes?

It is somehow offensive to contemporary man to consider the thought that a race of prehistoric men may have created a civilization the equal—if not the superior—of his own thousands, even millions, of years ago. Perhaps it is modern man's great pride that inhibits him from taking the time to examine such matters as "lost worlds" with any degree of seriousness.

There is something about the idea of an epoch before our own that seems to ring true in the inner reaches of the human psyche. In his *Worlds in Collision*, Immanuel Velikovsky wondered "... to what extent the terrifying experiences of world catastrophes have become part of the human soul and how much, if any, of it can be traced in our beliefs, emotions, and behavior, as directed from the unconscious or subconscious strata of the mind."

Various Amerindian peoples have legends which recount the evolution of mankind through a series of world, each of which is destroyed as man forgets the lessons of the Great Spirit and falls away to rely upon his own feeble devices. When this sad state of affairs comes to exist, the Great Spirit causes a time of Great Purification to cleanse the Earth Mother for a new epoch, a new world.

Hopi traditionalists recite their legends of the Four Worlds and warn of their prophecies, which state that a Great Purification will occur when people turn to material, rather than spiritual, matters; when evil ones set out to destroy the land and the life of the Hopi and other Amerindian brothers; when leaders of men turn to evil instead of the Great Spirit; when man has invented something which can fall upon the ground, boil everything within a great area, and turn the land to ashes where no grass will grow.

According to the traditional practitioners of Medicine Power who do not see this time of cleansing as being synonymous with the biblical Judgment Day—the ringing down of the cosmic curtain with a cataclysmic bang and the attendant weeping and gnashing of teeth. From my discussions with

Medicine people, it would seem that we also agree that this time of cleansing is the latest in a series of transitional periods which are necessary to man's spiritual evolution. We believe that mankind has been moving higher and higher in the frequency of his spiritual vibration, the raising of his consciousness. The vast majority of Medicine people and New Age visionaries do not see the Great Purification as a time of terrible judgment, but as a time of transcendence.

The legend of the Seven Worlds of the Seneca has been revealed to few outside of those who are a part of the oral tradition of the Iroquois nation. I am indebted to Twylah Nitsch—both for translating the legend and for permitting me to share it with my readers. She deliberated a great deal before she allowed me to copy the legend from her notebooks. "I agree with you that the time is now," she told me finally. "This must be shared."

To my non-Indian reader, I urge that this account not be read with the superficial superiority of a member of the dominant culture seeking mild diversion from a myth of a quaint, but primitive, people. There is deep symbolism contained within the legend of the Seven Worlds. I can only hope that you will permit yourself to open your spiritual channel and allow the full significance of these words to reach your higher self.

In the mind of Swen-i-o, the Creator, there was no time or place or even human beings—just Swen-i-o, the Creator, and endless space. A world of infinite splendor evolving in total tranquility began in the mind of Swen-i-o, our Creator.

Surrounding Swen-i-o was endless space.

The first act of Swen-i-o was to establish a place where all things that were to be born and all things that were to happen could be fulfilled. He named it Eternal Land.

The second act of Swen-i-o was to make a substance that contained the makings of patterns for all things to be created.

The third act of Swen-i-o was to make a substance that floated in a cloud-like maze before his presence. He named this the Field-of-Plenty.

The fourth act of Swen-i-o was to enclose the Field-of-Plenty within a globe where his creations would be manifested. He named this globe the First World.

In the mind of Swen-i-o the First World had been born, and it contained all the limitless creations that were to be. This is where it all began.

The first creation of the First World:

Swen-i-o took the substance from the Field-of-Plenty and arranged a pattern. He threw the substance around and around and caused the first sphere to be born. Swen-i-o breathed around the first sphere to give it power. Breathing upon it filled its spirit. The first sphere floated aloft in the Field-of-Plenty in a brilliant glow of light.

This was the Sun. It was the greatest light, because it was endowed with the greatest gift, the breath of the spiritual life.

The second pattern created by Swen-i-o:

Swen-i-o took the substance from the Field-of-Plenty and arranged a pattern. Rolling the substance around and around caused the second sphere to be born. Swen-i-o breathed upon the second sphere to give it power. Breathing upon it filled it with the Spirit. The second sphere floated aloft in the Field-of-Plenty in a glow of soft, shimmering light. Swen-i-o named it the Moon. The Moon is different in size because of its power. It is not the same.

The third pattern created by Swen-i-o:

Again Swen-i-o took the substance from the Field-of-Plenty, and rolling the substance around and around, caused the third sphere to be born. He breathed upon the third sphere to give it power. Breathing upon it filled it with the Spirit. The third sphere floated aloft in the Field-of-Plenty in a translucent sheen and was named Water. Water was different from the Sun and the Moon, because its power was not the same.

The fourth pattern created by Swen-i-o:

Again Swen-i-o took the substance from the Field-of-Plenty, and rolling the substance around and around, caused the third sphere to be born. He breathed upon the third sphere to give it power. Breathing upon it filled it with the Spirit. The fourth sphere floated aloft in the Field-of-Plenty in a bronze density, and he named it Earth. Earth is the smallest of the four creations, because its power was not the same. The fourth creation of Swen-i-o received the breath of life.

In the mind of Swen-i-o, the Earth had been divided into four segments, North, South, East, and West, with the colors defined.

Division of the First World:

In the mind of Swen-i-o, the First World would be divided into four segments. Swen-i-o breathed upon the First World, which contained the Sun, Moon, Water, and Earth as it floated in the Field-of-Plenty and caused it to divide into four segments.

Placing the first segment: The first segment was placed by Swen-i-o at the right of the First World, which was named East, where the sun rises. It was blanketed in the color yellow.

Placing the second segment: The second segment was placed by Swen-i-o at the top of the First World, which was named North, cold. It was blanketed in white.

Placing the third segment: The third segment was placed by Swen-i-o at the left side of the First World, opposite the East. It was named the West, where the sun sets. It was blanketed in the color red.

Placing the fourth segment: The fourth segment was placed in the opposite direction of the North, where it is warm. It was called South, and it was blanketed in blackness.

The decrees of Swen-i-o the Creator:

In the mind of Swen-i-o, the creations of the First World, the Sun, Moon, Water, and Earth, would receive their powers and abilities in decrees. The Sun shall travel the outer rim of the First World in all its brilliant splendor. It shall lift its head, a radiant gold, at a place named the East, passing through the North, a place of total whiteness; to the West, where its golden radiance shall turn to fiery red hues; sinking to rest in a place of total darkness. It was decreed the Sun shall be the Sun Father, whose light and great warmth shall help nourish the creations of the First World. He will be the chief of the Sun tribes (rays), whose light and warmth shall filter down to Earth. These were the first decrees to the Sun in the mind of Swen-i-o.

It was decreed the Moon, the lesser light, will travel the outer rim of the First World, glowing through its shimmering light, passing through the North, a place of total whiteness. The Moon shall send its light rays during the time the Sun rests. It shall manifest four changes upon its face: the new moon; the second moon; the third moon; the full moon, when everything is in full favor. The Moon shall be the chief of the Moon nation (stars). His light shall be the guardian of the night, with starlight trails making paths by a shimmering light. These are the decrees assigned to the Moon in the mind of Swen-i-o.

It was decreed the Water shall float on the First World, reflecting all the colors in the mind of the Creator. Water shall contain the substance in the Field-of-Plenty, where the creatures of the Creator shall evolve upon the Earth. It shall receive the breath of spiritual life, its greatest gift. It shall nurture the creations of the First World. These are the decrees assigned to the Water in the mind of Swen-i-o, the Creator.

It was decreed the Earth shall be the place where the Sun, Moon, and Water shall exert their greatest power. It shall receive gifts and abilities from the Great Spirit. It shall be known as Earth, for on its face all creation shall smile. These are the decrees assigned and fulfilled by Swen-i-o.

Creations of the First World:

In the mind of Swen-i-o the Creator, creatures were to be born, to evolve, and to live in Nature Land. Pattern after pattern was arranged from the substance in the Field-of-Plenty, all endowed with the breath of spiritual life. Taking the substance from the Field of Plenty, he sprinkled it throughout Eternal Land, causing its gifts and abilities to be born. Gifts and abilities drifted down from Nature Land to be received by Mother Earth. The Sun smiled on her and sent his rays to filter across her bronze face. In the mind of Swen-i-o, the waters of Nature Land began to evolve. The gifts shared by Mother Earth, nurtured by the power of the Sun and the power of the Water, were responsible for the evolution that led to the manifestation of man.

Migration of the First World:

Man emerged from the deep and walked upon the face of the Earth. He multiplied and established magnificent communities and superb cultures. He was not aware that, during this time, Swen-i-o had taken care of all of his needs, nor was he willing to learn. A very old legend unfolds the happenings that occurred in tracing the development of man from the beginning to his life of perfection:

The First World:

The nations of the First World emerged at the place where the Sun raised its head above the rim of the sky. At this place Mother Earth shared her gifts in great profusion. But the people at that time were not grateful for these gifts and caused a disease of waste to visit Nature Land. Swen-i-o looked at man and arranged a time for the first decree. A silence and great magnitude enveloped the minds of these early people, as a celestial voice spoke: "You are creatures of nature, created by me, to live always in true harmony. Wisdom, if learned, if balance of life. Breaking this law breeds misery and strife. The Great Spirit has spoken."

The people were impressed with the Great Revelation they had heard, and for a time they began to wonder how Nature Land was different. They soon found it very hard to follow the decree of the Great Spirit. As time passed, the decree was forgotten, and Swen-i-o arranged for a cleansing of the First World. He placed a blanket of protection over those creatures who honored his decree. He ordered the Sun to use its power in cleansing the First World. The power of the Sun caused the devastation of the First World.

The dawn of the Second World:
After the Sun's rays penetrated the Earth's surface and destroyed the remnants of the First World, in the mind of Swen-i-o can the dawn of the Second World. The lessons learned from the acts of the people who perished in the First World remained in the minds of those who were saved. Carefully they populated the Second World, and they reaped the benefits from the renewed gifts offered by Mother Earth. Their culture was superb, and it spread rapidly throughout the Second World. Migrations moved toward the North, a place of total whiteness, to the South, a place of total darkness, and with the nations adapting to the environment of these places. Their outer skin became faded where it was cold, and dark where it was hot. Migrations followed the Sun as he traveled the path of the Sky Dome from East to West.

Before long, it became evident that the people of the Second World were following in the footsteps of their predecessors who had inhabited the First World. The wanton waste of the gifts of Mother Earth and the careless imbalance of their lives brought on misery and strife that gripped the world in a disease of destruction. Those who still honored the decree of the Great Spirit were given a blanket of protection, and the cleansing of the Second World was begun.

Swen-i-o ordered the Sun to withdraw its warmth from the face of Mother Earth, leaving only the Moon to exert his power upon Nature Land. The lesser light of the Moon was unable to warm Mother Earth, because its power was not the same as the Sun's. A state of cold settled upon Nature Land. This caused the devastation of the Second World.

The Third World:
The massive cold had completely destroyed the remnants of the Second World. In the mind of Swen-i-o the time came for the dawn of the Third World. The Third World was inhabited by people and creatures with gifts and abilities that surpassed the gifts and abilities of the two previous worlds. They spread their influence along the path of the Sun, establishing magnificent civilizations and cultures, populating more than half of the world. Four races had evolved as a result of migrations: the white, the red,

the yellow, and the black—their complexions and physical characteristics having adapted to the environment in which they lived.

During the Third World the four races became more aware of the laws that governed Nature Land, and they made some effort to learn about its mystery. For this reason their civilization flourished for a longer period than the First and Second worlds. But in spite of their knowledge, they became forgetful, and they consistently brought disruption upon the gifts of Mother Earth.

For the third time, those who honored the decree of Swen-i-o were placed under the blanket of protection. Water, the third creation of Swen-i-o, was responsible for the cleansing of the Third World. Since this was in the mind of Swen-i-o, it was done. Water covered the face of Mother Earth. This caused the devastation of the Third World.

In the mind of Swen-i-o came the dawn of the Fourth World:

The migration of the Fourth World completed the population of the universe from East to West. The greatest span of existence was experienced by the people evolving in the Fourth World, because this world was the Middle World. The environmental experiences of the first three worlds had blended, causing an awakening to visit the minds of the people. Those whose evolvement had reached the awakening period were willing to share their knowledge with others. They began to keep records; but the greatest records were still in the minds of the generations who had lived under the "blanket of protection" and who still honored the decree of the Great Spirit. These people had evolved along the thread that connected them to Swen-i-o, the Creator.

During the Fourth World, the inhabitants became aware of the universal stream that revolved around the world, and they learned the wisdom of enlightenment. It was fully understood how they were evolving and how their spiritual lives guided them in their material existence. Some were aware of the happenings that occurred in the past, and some could even project happenings of the future. Through the minds of these people the Secret of the Ages was recorded.

Unfortunately, too many still pursued the materialistic path, spreading misery and doom among the inhabitants. A dreadful disease plagued the people of the Fourth World. They called it Fear. Its infection caused the nations to search for they-knew-not-what, bringing uncontrolled corruption and strife. For this reason, the cure for this disease was unknown to the inhabitants for a long period of time. More environmental experience and more lessons had to be learned before the disease could be understood. Instead of searching for the cause of the mystery of fear that would bring peace and happiness, they wantonly disrupted the gifts of Mother Earth.

It became evident that the Fourth World would have to undergo a cleansing period to renew the gifts of Mother Earth, just as the three previous worlds had. The cleansing of the Fourth World was exerted by the combined efforts of the Sun, the Moon, and Water upon Mother Earth. The Fourth World's corruption had been the greatest; therefore, her need for renewal, the greatest. The combined powers of the first three creations of Swen-i-o caused the devastation of the Fourth World.

In the mind of Swen-i-o was the dawn of the Fifth World:

The greatest strides in understanding took place in the Fifth World. The era of the awakening had become established, and man found self-satisfaction in sharing his gifts and abilities with others. The Records of the Ages were being uncovered and the false documents of man were being corrected. Man began to understand what he was searching for, and he opened his eyes to the purpose of his life. He searched within himself, and there he was.

The duration of the Fifth World was short compared to the previous worlds. Man had passed through many environmental experiences. His lessons were extremely difficult, but he had achieved self-mastery. He realized that there was much he could do if he used his knowledge to benefit mankind. Heretofore, he had reaped the punishment of destruction only through selfishness. However, he was not yet convinced of the duality of his nature regarding the function of his spiritual mind over the physical body. Wars within his attitudes and thoughts still festered in his mind, creating injustices upon the gifts of Mother Earth.

Man was having difficulty practicing the decree of Swen-i-o that had been revealed in the First World. Repeatedly, there had been messengers of the Great Spirit to remind the people of the wisdom of harmony. Yet they were unable to perpetuate their beliefs after the general disturbances of their way of life in the latter days of the Fourth World. Mother Earth was again in need of a renewal of her gifts. The cleansing was exerted by the power of the Sun and Moon and was completed in the mind of Swen-i-o, the Creator. This caused the devastation of the Fifth World.

The dawn of the Sixth World:

The Sixth World had the shortest evolvement period. It was the world that opened the eyes of man. He looked at himself and saw what he really was, but he lacked the ability to change it. He also recognized the necessity

148

of fitting into a pattern that functioned in unison with his world. As yet, he had not fully accepted the laws of nature as his guide. His life at times was still governed by his own selfish thinking. There had to be one more cleansing to renew the gifts of Mother Earth before man truly understood and could practice his purpose in life.

For all six worlds, he had wreaked havoc upon himself,
    his fellow man, and the creatures of Nature.
Now he stood at the threshold of perfection,
    awaiting the wisdom of the ages
    to penetrate his mind.

The cleansing of the Sixth World was exerted by the power of the Moon, followed by the heating properties of the Water, which paved the way for the dawn of the Seventh World.

The Seventh World:

In the Seventh World, the Happy Hunting Ground,
Man saw beauty everywhere.
He listened to the music of the Universe
And sang his part in the chorus.
He felt love for Swen-i-o and for his fellow man.
He shared his gifts and abilities with others.
He made the Seventh World a place of peace and happiness.

The final cleansing had been completed, and man's life was guided by a spiritual light, the same light that is in the mind of Swen-i-o, the Great Spirit. *Da naho naweh, Swen-i-o!*

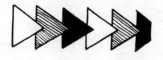

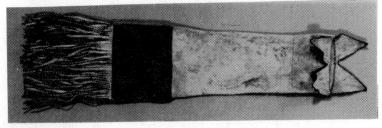

American Indians have been conducting vision quest for countless years. The "peace pipe" was often passed among the braves of the tribe for meditation purposes, and later on a dance was performed which would unite them with the spirit world. The Winnebago dance roach (above right) dates from the late 1800s, as does the Chippewa (above left) and Plains (bottom) pipes.
(Photo credits: Darryl Henning,
Luther College Anthropology Department)

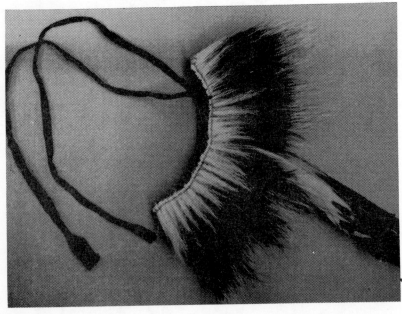

CHAPTER FIFTEEN

Conduct Your Own Spiritual Vision Quest

Here is a guided meditation that I have used at vision quests and Medicine Wheel gatherings throughout the United States and Canada. It is one that I have found very effective for leading groups into a simulated vision quest experience. It is one that you can use by prerecording your voice and by becoming your own guide through the experience. Or you may read it aloud to a trusted friend or loved one, and then have that same individual read it for you and lead you through the experience.

Enter a state of very relaxed frame of mind. When you have reached a deep level, when you have gone deep, deep, within—moving toward the very center of your essence—begin to tell yourself that you have the ability to visualize in your mind the conditions of your vision quest. Tell yourself that you have the ability to tap into the eternal transmission of universal truth from which you may draw power and strength. You have the ability to evolve as a spiritual being.

Visualize yourself as a native American man or woman on a vision quest. Focus your thoughts on your performance of some mundane, monotonous physical task. Perhaps like so many young native American men and women on a vision quest, you have found a small clearing in the forest which has a number of rocks of various sizes at one end of the nearly barren area. Pick up one of the rocks and carry it to the opposite side of the clearing. In your mind, see yourself carrying the rock. See yourself placing the rock down on the ground and turning around to get another rock. See yourself picking up a new rock, carrying it slowly to the other side of the clearing, and then another rock, and another, back and forth. Back and forth, over and over again.

Know and understand that you are performing this task for the sole purpose of depleting the physical self with monotonous exercise. Know and understand that you are distracting the unconscious mind with dull activity, that you are doing this to free the essential self within you, so that it can soar free of the physical body.

Feel now your body becoming very, very tired. Your body is feeling very heavy. It feels very, very dull. You have no aching muscles or sore tendons, but you are very, very tired. Your physical body is exhausted. See yourself lying down on the blanket to rest, to relax.

Slowly you become aware of a presence. Someone has approached you and has come to stand next to you. As you look up at the figure, you see

153

that it is a most impressive individual. It is a man who is looking at you with warmth and compassion.

And now you notice that he has been joined by a woman who is equally impressive, almost majestic in appearance. She smiles at you, and you feel somehow as if she stand before you enveloped in the Great Mother vibration.

Before you can open your mouth to speak, the man and the woman fade from your side. They simply disappear. You realize that they were spirits, that they came to you from the spirit world to demonstrate to you that, in many ways, on many levels, you have a subtle, yet intense, partnership with the world of spirits. The spirit man and spirit woman have given you a visual sign of the reality of this oneness with all spiritual forms of life.

You have but a moment to ponder the significance of the spirit visitation when you become aware of two globes of bluish white light moving toward you. You are not afraid, for you sense a great spiritual presence approaching you.

As you watch in great expectation, the first glow of bluish white light begins to assume human form. As the light swirls and becomes solid, you behold before you a man or a woman whom you regard as a whole person, a saint, a master, an illumined one. This figure, so beloved to you, gestures to your left side. As you turn, you are astonished to see a marvelous link-up with other holy figures from all times, from all places, from all cultures. You see that these personages from a beautiful spiritual chain from prehistory to the present—and without doubt, the future.

The holy one smiles benevolently, then bends over you and touches your shoulder gently. The holy one's forefinger lightly touches your eyes, your ears, then your mouth. You know within that this touching symbolizes that you are about to see and to hear a wondrous revelation, which you must share with others.

As the holy figure begins to fade from your perception, the second globe of bluish white light begins to materialize in human form. The entity that forms before you now may be very familiar to you. You man very likely have seen this entity in your dreams, for this is your guide. One who has always loved you just as you are. This is one with unconditional love who is concerned completely with your spiritual evolution. You feel totally relaxed, at peace, at one with your guide. You feel totally loved.

Your guide is now showing you something important. Your guide's hands are holding something for you to see. It is an object which you can

154

clearly identify, an object which will serve as a symbol that you are about to receive a meaningful and important teaching in your dreams. Whenever you see this symbol in your dreams, you will understand that an important and significant teaching will instantly follow.

The symbol fades from you sight, but you will remember it.

Now, in a great rush of color and light, you are finding yourself elevated in spirit. You know that your guide has taken you to a higher vibrational level. You have moved to a dimension where nonlinear, cyclical time flows around you.

From your previous limited perspective of Earth time, linear time, you are aware that you now exist in a timeless realm in eternal now. Stretching before you is something that appears to be a gigantic tapestry, a tapestry that has been woven of multi-colored living lights, lights that are pulsating, throbbing with life. The energy of the Great Spirit touches your inner knowing, and you are made aware that you are becoming one with the great pattern of all life. In a marvelous, pulsating movement of beautiful lights and living energy, your soul feels a unity with all living things.

You see before you now an animal, any animal. You become one with its essence. You become one with this level of awareness. Be that animal. Be that level of energy expression.

See before you a bird, any bird. Now become one with its essence. Become one with its level of awareness. Be that bird. Be that level of energy expression.

See before you a creature of the waters, any creature. Become one with its essence. Become one with its level of awareness. Be that marine creature. Be that level of energy expression.

See before you an insect—any insect crawling or flying. Become one with its essence. Become one with its level of awareness. Be that insect. Be that level of energy expression.

See before you a plant—any flower, tree, grass, or shrub. Become one with its essence. Become one with its level of awareness. Be that plant. Be that level of energy expression.

Know now that you are one with the unity of all plant and animal essence. Know now that you forever bear responsibility to all plant and animal life. You are one with all things that walk on two legs or four, with all things that fly, with all things that crawl, with all things that grow in the soil, or sustain themselves in the waters.

Listen carefully as your guide begins to tell you your secret name, your spirit name, the name that only you will know, that only you and your guide will share. It is the name by which your guide will contact you. Hear that name now.

And now your guide is showing you the image of an animal, a plant, a bird, a water creature, an image of one of the little brother or sisters other than humankind. Focus upon that creature. See its beauty. Become one with its beauty. Know that this animal, this creature, is now your totem—that symbol which will come to you often in dreams and represent the spirit of yourself on another level of reality.

See before you another person, a man, a woman, young or old. Go into that person. Become one with that person's essence. Become one with that person's level of awareness. Be that person. Be that level of energy expression.

Know now that it is never your to judge another expression of humankind. Know now that you have a common brotherhood and sisterhood with all of humankind. Remember always that you must do unto your brothers and sisters as you would have them do to you. Remember always that the great error is to in any way prevent another's spiritual evolution.

At this eternal second in the energy of the Eternal Now, at this vibrational level of oneness with all living things, at this frequency of awareness of unity with the cosmos, your guide is permitting you to receive a great teaching vision of something about which you need to know for your good and your gaining. Receive this great vision now.

You will awaken at the count of five, filled with memories of your great vision quest. When you awaken, you will feel morally elevated; you will feel intellectually illuminated. You will know that your spiritual essence is immortal. You will no longer fear death. You will no longer experience guilt or a sense of sin. You will feel filled with great charm and personal magnetism. You will feel better and healthier than ever before in your life, and you will feel a great sense of unity with all living things. One, two, three, four, five, awake!

A Chippewa medicine man, Sun Bear lectures widely on Indian philosophy, prophecies, Earth awareness and self-reliance in the New Age. He communicates with people about the coming earth changes and how humans can learn to live in harmony with each other and the Earth Mother. Below, he talks with Brad Steiger about future events.

CHAPTER SIXTEEN

New Tribes for a New Age

When I remarked to Rarihokwats, the Mohawk editor of *Akwesasne Notes*, that non-Indian youth were demonstrating by their very choice of dress—leather jackets, beaded headbands, moccasins, etc.—that there was something about the Indian life that was attractive to them, he replied that Indian-ness required more than the adoption of certain superficial aspects of Amerindian culture.

"You know," he went on, "we meet with a lot of the young people, and we talk with them. They are very often disappointed in us because we don't live up to their expectations of what we should be like. I think that in their rejection of their own culture, they have grabbed on to the nearest convenient replacement and are trying to become 'instant Indians.'

"I think what they really have to do is to retribalize. What they are doing now is a very individualistic kind of maneuver. What is required is even deeper than living with Nature: it is living as a *part* of Nature. Indians are one with Nature in a family kind of relationship. That is why all thing of Nature are expressed as brother or sisters, grandmothers and grandfathers. It is a close family relationship."

Ann Underwood had this to say about the Amerindian's tribal relationships: "Each person, from tiny child to the oldest person in the tribe, has his own function, his own place; and he never loses touch with Nature. Emotional disturbances and insanity are almost unknown among the traditional and tribalized Indian.

"I think the Indian method of child rearing is better than Dr. Spock's. We teach each that he is a person, that he has a respected place in his tribe, in his clan, in his family. He is told that he has certain responsibilities to face. He is taught to revere and respect his parents, his grandparents, the elder members of his clan and tribe; and he is taught to revere the Great Spirit. From the time a child is born, he knows exactly who he is, where he is, and what he is, and exactly what is expected of him. The child is as he is, and he is accepted on those terms, without ridicule, without being put down."

In his *We Talk, You Listen,* Vine Deloria, Jr., writes of the great source of strength which every Indian finds in the tribal structure. "Being inside a tribal universe is so comfortable and reasonable that it acts likes a narcotic," he informs his non-tribal readers. "When you are forced outside the tribal context you become alienated, irritable, and lonely. In desperation you long to return to the tribe if only to preserve your sanity."

161

Deloria sees our time as a process of retribalization, because "… we have become objects of a universe we do not understand and not subjects with a universe to exploit." Technological advancements disproportionate to man's humanistic growth have created an inhuman science that has displaced man from the smug master-of-his-fate role that has shaped a great deal of Western thought. The next step, as Deloria views it, is to create a new mythology and symbols to explain the new world:

"New concepts must define the questions of life, death, and society which are derived from the nature of man as a tribal animal. The individualistic rationalism that has brought Western man to the present cannot preserve his sanity for him in the future.

"We have come from an oral culture through a literate culture and then suddenly been thrust beyond the literate culture by our communications media into a qualitatively different oral culture again. This generation of young people has been raised on television and has lived a continuous existence instead of the broken and alienated existence which plagued their elders. The categories of existence are different for the generations, and the older generation cannot stand the freedom which the young exhibit."

Deloria recognizes the Woodstock Nation as a new distinct minority group in our culture, a minority group that has rejected the older equality of individual mythology in favor of group tactics and group goals. He senses a desperate need for "traditional structures, concepts, and mythologies to provide a means of translating ideas and values between generations and between whites and non-whites."

If the new minority groups do not quickly translate their "harmless group feeling" into a demand for "recognition of the sovereignty of their groups," Deloria foresees their dissolution and destruction. In his opinion: "Any future coalition of groups for change must adopt Indian formats. The desire to have spectacular demonstrations and disruptions must give way to a determination to maintain the community at all costs. This can only be possible by creation of new mythologies internal to each group in a manner similar to contemporary tribal understandings of the history of the people."

Deloria tells us that we have a chance to structure a new cosmopolitan society within the older North American society, "but it must be done by an affirmation of the component groups that have composed American society. We can no longer build upon a denial of everything that makes a person himself."

162

We must, in his estimation, renew various symbols in order to restore communications between generations and combine the older symbols with a "new vision of the nature of man" which has been achieved by "creating a new mythology of creation itself."

"The current fascination with ecology is one key to the new mythology," Deloria informs us, "because it attempts to understand the real natural world as a part of us and we as a part of it.... We must return to and understand the land we occupy. Communications have made the continent a part of the global village. The process must be reversed. The land must now define the role communications can play to make the country fruitful again."

There are a number of communes throughout the United States and Canada that provide living substantiation for the observations Deloria makes in regards to the youth of the Woodstock Nation minority seeking to restore ancient symbols and to combine them with new mythologies and a new vision of the nature of man. Many of these New Age communes combine a dedication to the Cosmic Christ, a belief in the Brotherhood of Man, and the practice of Essenic Christianity, with an observance of the old traditions of the Amerindians. Whether these new tribal structures actually provide us with a preview of how man will live, work, and worship in the New Age or whether they represent experiments in counterculture lifestyles, they are worthy of our examination and consideration.

White Bear, the Hopi prophet, is spiritual advisor to the Brotherhood of the Sun, which is located at 3,000 feet in the mountains overlooking Santa Barbara, California and the Channel Islands, while Norman Paulson is its guiding force and strength, both is founder and its guru. Paulson has long brown hair, a full beard, and a husky build that fills out the simple work clothes that he wears. Although he is a mystic, a visionary, his hands and his physique give evidence of the years that he spent as a bricklayer, a carpenter, and now, a tiller of the soil.

Norman Paulson: *I think it is a wonderful thing that the Indian are reviving their old culture and their old ways, because the truth of the Great Spirit, or the Living God, is in every religion and in every race.*

I think the Hopi are the greatest example of brotherhood and living together in harmony with the Spirit that we have today. The Hopi settled in that remote area they call home because they did not want to become spiritually lax in a fertile climate and in a fertile ground. They wanted to depend upon their attunement with the life-force to grow their food and to produce the moisture necessary.

White Bear gave us Hopi seed for squash and corn. It produced pretty good this summer on what we call Lemuria Ranch.

The Hopi tradition and our way of life is very much the same, even to your meditation. I haven't looked too extensively into the other Indian tribes, but there seems to be a similarity in religious beliefs. It appears to me, though, that the Hopi seems to have kept his traditions together more than any other tribe.

I think the White Brother is happening right now here on the West Coast. I think it is a generation of young people, as well as older people, who recognize the basic values of life and who wish to live in harmony with the world and with nature. The meaning of the White Brother and the Red Brother is already taking place. The Indians are astonished because there seems to be a generation of whites who not only want to live as the Indians have for thousands of years, but who are doing it.

Of course we do not condemn everything our society has produced. We believe in taking things that don't pollute and the good that man has created into a new environment, discarding those things that do pollute our bodies and our souls. With the guidance of White Bear, we are seeking to form our harmonious relationship with nature. We are able to show a number of these things in the movie that we produced, Empire of the Sun.

We selected that title for our movie because we believe that there was once a continent in the Pacific that was called Mu, which all the legends of the Hopi definitely state they migrated from. Mu was known as Empire of the Sun, and we feel that our movie is about the resurrection of a way of life that lasted over two hundred thousand years without any wars. We are trying to show that this true brotherhood can be accomplished again.

You mentioned that your meditation techniques were similar to those of the Hopi. Could you elaborate just a bit on these techniques, please?

Norman Paulson: *My feeling is that the pillar of fire that Moses was talking about is something that just about everyone at the Brotherhood of the Sun is aware of. We are using the ancient form of meditation which has to do with the aperture at the crown of the head. My own experiences have shown me that this method evolved out of the continent of Lemuria, and the*

Hopi carried it with him when he came into North America. The Tibetans that I have met use the same type of meditation.

I experienced the raising of kundalini after five years of continuous effort through Yogananda's method of meditation. At the same time I experienced the descending of an inner spiritual sun. It had to do with the crown of the head and the energy that has come into the crown of the head. Both forces met in the heart. The consciousness centered in the heart and the body experienced the breathless state, the stopping of the heart, and the death trance. I experienced it for five hours the first time. My coming back into the body had to do with descending out of the burning light of inner sun, down through the crown of the head. Through this experience, I began to practice my own method of meditation, which involved receiving this life through the crown of the head.

Moses said when he led the children of Israel that there was a pillar of fire by night and a cloud by day. Everywhere we look through the ancients we find that the pillar of fire and the cloud have to do with the higher vibratory energy. My own experience was an evolution of a series of live in Lemuria, which I remembered in my years at Yogananda's.

After becoming aware of the Hopi and their migrations, I was able to fit my own experiences to theirs; and at the right time, White Bear arrived at the Brotherhood and he gave me confirmation.

In a vision, I was shown the offshore islands around Santa Cruz Island, and I was told that these lands were going to be for the new children of the New Age. The Empire of the Sun was rising. It was stretching forth its hand from the sea to reclaim certain land for the children of the New Age. These children are white Indians or the lost White Brother, for whom they have been looking from Quetzalcoatl to the Hopi, to the Inca to the Maya. These lost white children are now reincarnated and large numbers of them have been gathering on the West Coast of the United States. Many of them are unaware of why they are here and who they are.

I was taken to our ranch, for which we have just acquired another big property in the wilderness. A standard with a full sun disk was driven in the ground on a four-cornered square. On the standard were the words Empire of the Sun. Spirit said these lands belonged to the children of the New Age. They will extend from here to Hopi lands, south to Mexico City, north to Mount Shasta. They will include all the Pacific islands and Hawaii.

Spirit referred to the Empire of the Sun as being the Old Garden of Eden. There were twelve tribes originally assembled there. The twelve tribes *are the twelve vibrations emanating from the sun of our galaxy. These twelve vibrations of people are scattered on solar systems throughout our galaxy. When a certain solar system has reached a point nearest the higher vibration, they all reassemble. Right now we are coming out of the Dark Age, and the tribes are beginning to reassemble. This is the first indication of the return of the Garden, or the spiritual consciousness.*

My meeting with White Bear is in recognition of the White Brother. White Bear has now fulfilled the prophecy that his mother told him, that in the last days he would go to the Hawaiian Islands, the last stepping-stones from Lemuria to the New World.

It all comes together. I can show you that the Tibetan prayer wheel evolved out of Lemuria exactly the same as the Hopi medicine wheel. It shows a 24,000-year cycle of our sun and planets moving around the inside of the zodiac. Every 24,000 years all these things take place.

When Lemuria existed, there were twelve tribes, basic brotherhoods; they were different races and they looked different because of the vibratory regions of space in which they came. When the migrations from Lemuria began, some went east and some went west. The white Indian went toward the rising sun. The White Brother migrated into the land of the Incas and the Aztecs. From there he went into Atlantis and from there to Greece and parts of Egypt. The White Brother was the roots of Abraham, the Jew.

When Moses was in Egypt and said that the Garden lay eastward in Eden, he knew it wasn't in India, because Egypt was trading with India. He knew the Garden was further east.

The Essenes were a reincarnated group that set up the master vortex for the coming of Christ. To set up a master vortex, you have to have all twelve sides of the zodiac together, each illuminated in the same vibration—each one with his vortex; each one receiving his vibrations; preferably, each one born in the center of the zodiacal sign, not in the beginning or the end.

When the right twelve are assembled and receiving, you have the master power. But you only have half of it. This is what Jesus was trying to assemble out the Essene movement. Unfortunately, they didn't have women, which would have given them the other half. They lost the ability to bring the whole truth, the whole realization. But now in this age we can do it.

166

Right now we have all twelve at Sunburst Farms, and the signs align, as in Mary's (Mrs. Paulson) and my case. We are both Aquarians, our moons match, Both Sagittarius. We have been together from the beginning.

Now, this planet is at the threshold of the Garden. Men and women are going to realize their true divine nature, and they are going to ascend, instead of descend, with their energy.

We are overpopulated; there are no homes, no food; people are dying in the street; because man went into the house of lust with his own desires. Now we can come out. The true way to live is by knowing the Infinite Self, the Living God.

With meditation and the establishment of the Pillar of Fire, the life and the knowledge and the vision of your own inner sun, you will know how to enter the Aquarian Age.

The Bear Tribe, led by Sun Bear, a Chippewa medicine man, is more traditionally American Indian and has fewer Eastern and non-Indian metaphysical elements incorporated into its structure than does the Brotherhood of the Sun. The Bear Tribe is familiar with the ancient prophecies that foretold of a time when refugees from white society would come to the red man as lost brothers, and they have invited non-Indian peoples to join them and to learn to develop harmony with Nature. Sun Bear regards the Bear Tribe as the first new Indian tribe of this century, and he emphasizes its principles of returning to the land and to the traditional Amerindian way of life.

Sun Bear: *In our twelve years of existence, we have become both national and international. We lecture throughout the world on Native philosophy and prophecies, earth awareness, and self-reliance. We give seminars at our home base near Spokane, Washington, and in other location. We feel that much of our medicine is communicating with people about this time of earth changes and about how people can live more in harmony with each other and with Earth Mother. At our home community, we have twenty or more people who run our farm and help with teaching others about self-reliance.*

Our home base is on a mountain that was known to the Spokane Indians as Vision Mountain. We conduct vision quests for people here, since we feel that it is essential for people today to get in contact with their own visions. We do a lot of work tying together various groups and individuals.

We now sponsor at least four medicine wheel gatherings each year, in which a thousand or more people come together to build a medicine wheel to celebrate the Earth and all of their relations upon her. At these gatherings, we bring together about a dozen teachers to share with the participants. We also do a lot of work with trading and bartering and with helping other communties to become more self-reliant. We feel that it is essential for people to know that there are alternatives to the economics of America.

When we first started the Bear Tribe, we held out our hands on a "bring your poor, your discontented" basis. We accepted people wholeheartedly, and we also accepted them at their word.

But a lot of people were not sincere in that theirs was a lip thing. They were rip-offs. Instead of learning that the first step toward spiritual balance is to work the land and to learn love and harmony, they just wanted to shake the rattle and sing the songs. There was no real commitment or love to anything.

Would you say that because of their non-Indian cultural conditioning these people simply wanted spiritual blessings instantly, without having to apply any real effort?

Sun Bear: *Yes, they wanted their religion in a capsule. The other thing was that, in terms of a real relationship of living, the American society has dealt with people to the point where they aren't able to build a spiritual discipline. These are just two of the problems that I have observed in the twelve years that I have been working with the Bear tribe. According to the way I interpret my medicine, I must offer it to the non-Indian people as well as the Indian.*

Throughout my work with the Bear tribe, I have offered my medicine to people of all races because in my vision I saw a blending of Indian and non-Indian people. Sometimes both Indians and non-Indians have objected to my working with people of all races, but I feel that we must all learn to come together in unity, to work together in harmony on the Earth Mother with a real love relationship and a sincere sense of responsibility for ourselves and for the Earth Mother.

I agree with you that both Indian and non-Indian peoples might benefit from the heritage our nation has in the Amerindian culture. Could you tell me what you feel the

traditional ways offer to modern man in this new age of ever-rising awareness?

Sun Bear: *Well, knowledge never changes; it remains a strong and continuing thing. Indian medicine and the power behind it is very much alive today. It has not vanished; it is not antiquated. To the traditional Indian people, we see more of a strong need for it today than ever before. We see a continent being devastated by people who are stupidly trying to get rich quick by raping the Earth Mother. We feel that it is basic for the survival of this nation that people learn much of our traditions, much of the knowledge that we have to teach.*

Unfortunately, too many of the non-Indian on this continent have no real spiritual conviction. Too many practice a "Sunday religion," a mouth thing, not a heart thing. This shows in their lives. There is nothing real about this social kind of worship. We traditional Indian people feel that if your religion is a real thing, it should work for you every day.

When we make our prayers, we ask for medicine to work for us. We expect the rain to come tomorrow, not six months from now.

When the non-Indians prays for peace, he waves the sword in the other hand. They have no real commitment toward it. I make no prayers for peace for this nation, because I see its destruction by its own stupidity.

I regard myself as a humanitarian. I love my fellowman-Indian, black or white or whatever. Those whom I call brother or sister are those who share the same philosophy and respect for the Earth Mother and for each other as human beings.

We traditional people consider ourselves keepers and protectors of the Earth Mother. We have a responsibility not only to this generation, but to all generations to come. That is why we are concerned over the environment, concerned over the natural resources. We feel that in other lands across the world, there are other people of ancient origin who have labored in a manner similar to our work—people who are keepers and protectors.

I believe in pride and in Indian culture and in our traditional way of life. I am proud that we have been able to retain this necessary wisdom. But I don't think of this as a racist thing. I don't want to kill the white man or anybody else. I feel very strongly against this. I feel as strongly against the Indians who destroy as I feel sorry for the Indian people who carry a wine jug in their hands and tell me that they are traditional Indians.

A lot of people who came as seekers of Indian medicine are people who only want these powers for themselves. They don't intend to use the medicine for the benefit of other people.

I had a man come to me one time who wanted me to teach him medicine ways. He was another one who was in a hurry to get hold of the rattle, you know. I asked him what he wanted medicine for. He said that he had studied Yoga and that he had studied other things. "I just want to know it for myself," he said.

I told him that I couldn't teach him. I felt that it would be a waste of time.

If the man had been willing to use medicine in harmony and to work with our people and our groups, then it would have been another thing. He was like so many people who approach their religion for selfish reasons. These people want to save their souls from hell, or they want to be sure they get themselves to heaven. But both reasons are for themselves alone.

Too many of these people who come to the reservations to drop off their little boxes of old clothes are doing it to make brownie points with the Sky God. They are not really doing it for the benefit of someone else. They are doing it for themselves. This is the arrogance of all these people who are going along on a trip just for the free ride. The reality of it is that if humanity is to develop and to evolve into better balance, then somewhere along the line, we have to put away all this arrogance.

In the Bear Tribe, we have three rules we ask of those who come to join us:

First, we tell them they aren't coming to do their thing, they are coming to do our thing.

In order to walk in balance and harmony with each other on the Earth Mother, there is to be no liquor—because we have seen destruction both of our own people and other people due to liquor—and there are to be no hard drugs.

There is to be no possessiveness. That does not mean they do not have responsibilities toward things that are around them. But they should look at land, vehicles, livestock, as things they can share.

You see, the time has to come when humanity walks not as men and women, but as human beings. We don't want any of the jealousy barriers that cause the same sicknesses that builds wars between nations and the all the rest of it.

170

The medicine that I offer through the Bear tribe and that I believe in, is not a medicine of the Sioux of yesterday or the Chippewa of yesterday. It is a medicine of today, as well as a medicine of tradition. This is the medicine that I see as going to have to bring the balance between the races on the Earth Mother.

Some other Indian may say, "That is not what the Sioux believe," or, "That is not what the Chippewa believe," or, "That is not what I believe."

Well, then, that is true. It is not. It is what I see, what my medicine has shown to me at this time.

I have had problems with some of the people who are with me, who still have not fully found the ability to comprehend what my medicine is about. But if you are to live out in the hills with a group of people, you are going to have to get it together there. You are going to have to be like the traditional Indian has always said: "They who walk with a good balance carry the law within their hearts."

We didn't need a billy club on every corner before the white man came, and we were able to survive on this land for thousands of years. We didn't need the corner policeman to beat our heads in.

If this nation is to grow as a true nation of brothers and sisters, then everyone must learn to walk with a good balance and to carry the law in his heart.

Of partial Cherokee ancestry, the author's wife, Francie Steiger, sees our
planet evolving into a higher vibration so that all things that once issued
forth from the Source that is God may return
to pure energy. As an internationally known mystic she has
accurately predicted many future events.

CHAPTER SEVENTEEN

The Coming Great Purification and Earth Changes

As I travel about the country lecturing to groups and visiting with Medicine people and New Age visionaries, I am continually met by men and women who attempt to define a sense of urgency that has caused them to quit good jobs so that they may await they know not what. Older people as well as younger people seem haunted by a foreboding of impending, major changes which are about to transform society and humanity into something other than they presently encompass.

Some interpret these vibrations, these foreshadowings of some dramatic future event, to be the Day of Judgment which is promised in the Bible, a day in which the "elect" will be removed from the Earth and the "condemned" will be left behind to perish. Because of my own visions and those of the Medicine people and New Age prophets, I do not see this coming super-event to be the end of the world. I do believe, however, that we are entering the latest in a series of transitional periods which are necessary for mankind's spiritual evolution.

As Dallas Chief Eagle phrased it, "From the point of view of Indian theology, there is no such thing as the end of the world. There are upheavals, colossal upheavals, but no great end of the world."

"I look at the Earth Mother as a relation of mine," Chief Eagle went on. "I don't think people realize that our Mother Earth has a nervous system, just like a human body. I don't believe our fair Earth Mother can take any more of the abuse that it has been forced to suffer by man. And when the nervous system of this planet is upset, it has to readjust itself, just like any other organism. The Earth Mother has to make its own adjustments and retain its balance. And when it does this, there will be catastrophes on its surface ... and mere man is going to suffer.

I agree with Chief Eagle and both ancient and contemporary Amerindian prophets that there will be great physical cataclysms attendant with this transitional period, this time of Great Cleansing, but I believe that they will be as nothing compared to the psychological cataclysms which will be experienced by those men and women who have not prepared themselves for the coming change in consciousness. Those people who are today ignoring the abundant cultural omens of change, those who will not restructure their methods of thoughts, those who will not release their hold on material reality, will be literally shattered.

As I have said in my sharings with groups throughout the United States, I fear mass suicides, incredible epidemics, nervous breakdowns among those men and women who refuse to recognize the ever-expanding, ever-widening cracks in this material dimension of being, and who resist acknowledging the sensate consensus of reality for the flimsy construct that it really is.

Hopi traditionalists are storing food and water for the coming Great Purification. They have been told that there will a terrible famine sometime soon—no longer than two or three years in the future. Canned and dehydrated foods, seed, kerosene lamps, bottled water, and water purification tablets are being put aside in carefully concealed caches.

Sun Bear told me that his Bear tribe is judiciously putting away stores of food and survival materials in the manner of the Hopi. "According to one of the ancient prophecies," he said, "the Great Purification will come after the white man has built a house in the sky. We believe that prophecy refers to Skylab."

When I asked Sun Bear if there might be anything that the System might do to stave off the approaching cleansing of the Earth Mother, he shook his head and replied:

"We know that it has already happened in the Spirit World. Soon Spirit Time will become our time, and it will happen here on Earth. There is nothing man can do to stop it. The Earth Mother will shake fleas off her back, just as a dog rids itself of its parasites. When the Cleansing has occurred, good people of spiritual awareness will build a better world."

What about all the brothers and sisters, who for one reason or another, just cannot get out of the cities to prepare for the Great Cleansing?

Sun Bear: *You are asking for kind words, and all I can say is that the reality is that, at some point, the cities will not be places where people can survive. The whole structuring of a city is anti-nature. Anti-nature is anti-anything that is real. The Earth Mother is going to cleanse itself. The people are going to have to cleanse themselves by getting rid of past concepts of things and by coming in harmony with the land.*

It will be important to find people to whom you can relate—a group that come together and offers harmony. But human beings have to regenerate their mental outlook so that they can come together in complete harmony.

And harmony cannot come alone from going up on a mountaintop and doing the bit of contemplating on your navel and thinking that is all there is to it. That kind of mysticism is selfish, because you are only riveting into yourself.

Go up and spend your time fasting and take in knowledge, but remember that all the great Medicine leaders of the past, leaders like Crazy Horse, were asking, "How can I best serve my people?" Unless knowledge is for some purpose, like helping you to find a better balance or helping you work together with your brothers and sisters, it doesn't mean a thing.

If you can embrace one another with a real love and a real sense of responsibility for each other, then you can really go up on the mountaintop or the Medicine lodge or the meadow and make true Medicine. You will even be able to make crops grow. That is a reality.

The old Medicine people of the Pawnee used to plant corn in the middle of winter. They would sing Medicine songs and the corn would grow up in one day. They used to prove this in front of the great American generals, who would come out and see it done. There are forces powerful enough so that if you can link up with them, they can do tremendous things.

This System is destroying itself because of the selfish pitting of people against one another. The only way we can heal people is individually. There is no way to heal this nation, because it is dead. It will be destroyed. Not by brothers wanting to take revenge on the System, but by much more powerful forces than revolution.

The only way anyone will survive the Great Purification is to cleanse himself as much as he can, so that he can function as a true brother who will live with others in harmony. This is the most important Medicine for survival. This nation is being destroyed because of the energies of hate, selfishness, and destruction that it has created. Now those energies have reversed their field and they are coming down on us.

And this destruction is too far set in motion to be halted?

It has already been sealed. The spirits that we have spoken to have said that it has already happened. It is sealed. This is a thing like we are on a continuous time belt, and we can't see tomorrow, because from our little point of view, we haven't gotten there yet. In the spiritual universe, tomorrow is already here. This is sealed and no changes can be made.

Page Bryant is a nationally recognized psychic, teacher, and lecturer, who currently resides with her husband, New Age artist Scott Guynup, in Colorado. Page has appeared as a guest speaker at many of the Bear tribe's

Medicine Wheel gatherings, and she has become extremely involved with the learning of Medicine ways.

In a series of visions, Page was shown the seven chakras of the Earth Mother:

The base chakra, the kundalini of the Earth, is located in the Pacific Ocean, and is known as the "ring of fire." This is the opening in the etheric body of the planet that allows the "fire of Spirit" to permeate the planet and therefore raise its consciousness ... As the Earth Mother evolves (she is magnetic and feminine), this "ring of fire" area will provide the energy for evolution and spiritual growth ...

I was also told by my Source that the Solar Plexus of the Earth Mother is the area covered by the central part of the Atlantic Ocean, a magnetic chakra of energy. I understand that the Solar Plexus, located in the navel of man, is the seat of one's emotions, the sensing center in the body. So is the Atlantic to the Earth. (This would also have been the site of the ancient continent known as Atlantis, and the inhabitants of this land were supposed to be highly developed in their "magnetic" or psychic powers and their sense of perception....)

The spleen chakra is in the area of Alaska, the northernmost United States and western and northernmost Canada, as well as the fringes of Siberia. This is the chakra that deals with cleansing and purification ... and these are clean and pure lands, touched only by hands of men who are in balance with the Earth....

The heart chakra of the Earth is located in the area of the United States known as the "Four Corners," a place where the states of New Mexico, Arizona, Colorado, and Utah are joined together. The joining forms the ancient symbol of the equal-armed cross, a symbol of nature and of manifestation. The heart center is the love center, the christen center of the planet. This center, which represents brotherhood, is situated on Indian land.

The throat chakra is located in the area of land mass that we call Puerto Rico ... another magnetic center. We think of the throat as the tool of speech and communication; and, therefore, it is interesting to note that this area is the physical home (at Aerocibo) of the largest radio telescope in the world—a scientific tool that serves as an offer of communication to the vast reaches of the universe.

The brow center of the planet is in the area of Tibet, Mongolia, and China. Through the civilizations that have developed in these lands and through the efforts of the Earth herself, the spiritual eye has been, and still is, in the process of development.

The crown chakra is said to be located in the center of the Gobi Desert, a vast wasteland, but the site of Shamballa energies, the divine vibrations of the entire sphere.

... I understand that the Earth is a Temple of Experience ... My quest has only begun. I work now to know how the Native Americans lived on her so well. I work now to share with people all over the land through my radio broadcasts the knowledge that our brothers and sisters of various tribes knew so well. I give thanks to the Great Spirit that there are a few of the Indian wise ones who are coming forward during this preparation period for another initiation of the planet. I thank them for sharing their knowledge and for the opening up the path to all humankind, so that we all might share in this understanding of our Home.

With the Great Purification just around the time loop, might we not expect some assistance and guidance from the Spirit World?

Twylah told me that she was certain that there were spiritual hands trying to lead the way.

"We will see more and more Indian ghosts walking across the land," Chief Eagle said. "They are coming back to touch the white man's heart. They are coming back not only for the Indian's sake, but for the sake of the entire globe."

Sun Bear commented, "All over this land are the guardians, or keepers, of the Earth Mother. We traditional people are the living visible guardians of this land. The others, the ghost, are the keepers and protectors over us. There are guardian spirit forces all over the land, but there are also spiritual its of destruction about.

"The destroyers are all over now, too; and you can see the expression of the energies they have created. There is a violent spirit that hovers over this land like a cloud. These destroyers will soon unleash their entire strength. The only people who will retain their balance will be the people who have linked into their minds the things that are really solid and true. These people will survive because they will keep themselves away the centers of strife and destruction. This is a headless nation now. Before too long, it will be devoured by the things it has created.

In an issue of *Survival,* a publication of the Church and School of Wicca in New Bern, North Carolina, Gavin and Yvonne Frost, Celtic traditionalists, discussed a number of prophecies relevant to the coming Earth changes:

Edgar Cayce " predicted in 1943 that in the next 30 or 40 years the earth will be broken up in the western portion of America. The greater portion of Japan must go into the sea ... Land will appear of the east coast of America. There will be a shifting of the poles.... The sinking or rising of the Mediterranean is given as one pointer to the start of these events.

This change in the Mediterranean area may be that mentioned in the Old Testament in several places. Zechariah 14, v. 4: "And his feet shall stand in that day upon the Mount of Olives ... [which] shall cleave ... towards the east and toward the west." V.8: "Living waters shall go out from Jerusalem, half of them toward the former sea, and half of them toward the hinder sea."

Ezekiel had a vision of fishermen standing on the shores of the Dead Sea, harvesting great quantities of fish. At the moment, will live in the water of the Dead Sea. However, an earthquake which would split the Palestine would cause the water of the Mediterranean to flow right through to the Red Sea on the other side. The prophecy has clearly not occurred yet, and could be tied in with the Cayce forecast.

In the Writings of the Ba'hai religion, the same prophecy occurs concerning America. The Eskimos and Canadian Indians will be the future leaders of the people of this country, the Writings state.

My wife Francie, the internationally known mystic, who is of French-Scots-Cherokee ancestry, see our planet evolving into a higher vibration so that all things that once issued forth from the Source may return to pure energy. In her book *Reflections from an Angel's Eye* and in our *Star People* series, Francie has made the following observations and predictions concerning the coming period of transition and cleansing:

The elevating of Earth's vibrational energies in the world of matter will affect every level of its inhabitants—spiritually, mentally, physically. Since we are matter as well, we must also be ready for our return to energy, for our attainment of a higher vibration of more harmonious energies.

* * * * *

In the beginning, the Source devised a Plan that would permit it to grow, to expand, to increase in complexities, and thereby to experience life in a myriad of forms and dimensions. The Source caused countless beings to exist on many levels of reality. Each being in its own level gathers the fruit acquired from its particular experience, thereby increasing and elevating its vibrations, and thus evolving ever upward in its return to the Source.

* * * * *

Cataclysmic events will occur, not because mankind has been wicked and sinful and must now receive collective punishment, but because of certain cyclic events which shape our planet's geological and vibrational structure. In the approaching cycle, the polarities will reverse, and all matter on Earth will rise to a higher vibrational frequency.

No single member of humankind lives long enough to observe these cycles, but from the viewpoint of the cosmic intelligences, all major occurrences come in cycles. All matter is energy, and energy comes to us in waves.

We will experience the birth throes of the New Age for approximately twenty more years, wherein there will exist earthquakes and floodings, with their terrible shadows of famine and pestilence. As conditions stand today, the channelings have indicated that the New Age will occur in 1999, but because its advent is due to an accumulation of polarized electromagnetic energies, the precise time is not yet determined.

* * * * *

Those who live on the coastal regions of all countries will be in danger during the time of transition, which will accelerate in the 1980s.

The entire Earth will experience many disasters—quakes, floodings, splittings, and famine. An inner shift of energies, of polarities, will occur, shaking our very foundation. Those who seek to live by the Spirit must be strong in the years which lied ahead. All will be affected by these many catastrophes in varying degrees.

It has been shown to Francie that thoughts and actions are vibrational in nature. Since they are magnetically governed, they are attracted to either the positive or negative poles of Earth. Here, they accumulate, until they reach such a degree of intensity that the tension affects weakened areas which

181

normally exist in the Earth's crust. Because these accumulated vibrations affect all of matter, the mounting tensions will cause these weakened areas to become high-risk places.

Francie's vision of the time of Earth Changes and cataclysms took the form of a great three-pronged split that extended down from the north polar region:

In the manner of a three-taloned claw, this will gravely affect the Earth's crust and will cause considerable devastation. This three-taloned claw will encompass half of the world, and will indicate areas of great tension and stress.

The first talon will cross diagonally downward over the eastern region of the Soviet Union, then lower into eastern China.

The second talon will stretch diagonally downward across central Canada and into mid-California.

The third talon will cross central Greenland, from northwest to east, move downward into the Mediterranean and into Northern Africa.

These are the paths of the three-taloned claw. These are the places where major tensions will exist during the coming electromagnetic shifting of the polar regions.

Areas on either side of the three gripping talons will be affected, but all land near the coastal regions will suffer to an even greater degree with quakes, floods, great winds, and climatical changes. Those areas farther inland will be the least afflicted.

The time of great devastation has occurred on Earth twice before. On the first occasion, there were only animals on the planet. On the second occasion, people suffered the catastrophes, and many earlier cultures and civilizations were destroyed.

These great devastations are vibrational, accumulative events which are natural to this planet. No one knows the exact time the fast-approaching devastation will begin, but it will be soon, quite likely before 1999. (Francie was told that in order to discover the "safe" places during the coming cataclysms, one must first "feel" and meditate upon those areas which are the strongest. When choosing a place to live, one must select a solid area that can withstand great strain.)

Feel those areas which emanate the least vibrations. Study the topography of all regions and ascertain those which are the driest. Areas near bodies of water of any major proportion are in danger. Water in vast amounts will shift, take different courses, different directions, and be jarred from present boundaries. The amount of miles inland which will be considered a safe area will depend upon the size of the body of water it is near.

Even in the driest of areas, far from water, the present emanations existing suggest splittings, shiftings, settlings, and major cave-ins. These ground shifts will occur ont only in regions near the three-pronged strain, but in particular areas that were once seabeds. where underground caverns now exist. These regions will not be able to withstand the shakings, the shiftings, and the strain.

The safest regions primarily will be the desert regions—as long as one takes into consideration those areas which are presently desert, but are dangerous due to their proximity to large bodies of water.

The following, then, are the safest areas: major parts of Arizona; the southern part of Colorado, the large, western area of New Mexico, and the northern region of Mexico. Inland Australia is safe, as is mid-Arabia, the southwest Soviet Union, and the driest region of northwest China.

You, who are Star People, permit your "mark on the forehead," the so-called "third eye," to lead you to safety. As you keep in mind the regions above, meditate upon the area of thought that feels safe to you. You are aware that the dangerous emanations and regions do exist. Your inner guidance will help you make your final decision in ascertaining your safest place.

All people of Spirit must be ready to share their energies during this time of travel. The Star People's capacity to love will be greater during this time, as they observe the birth throes of a New World of higher vibrational frequencies.

Love must be the guiding force in all that we undertake. The next two decades will be among the most important that humankind has ever faced. The entire species is about to face its moment of decision.

* * * * *

And again I saw that, upon their death, those people who vibrate with the most harmonious of energies rise to become as one, enjoining with God. In the end the Source is magnified, glorified, increased in greatness and in complexity, and thus permitted to experience life in a myriad of forms and dimensions in the realm of matter, thereby gaining new energies from all of existence.

I believe the coming transition will be one of change for the entire species, an evolutionary leap forward for man on both a biological and spiritual level, a move from what we now understand as humanhood to a higher consciousness in a new mode of being.

Our new generation of mystics are very reluctant to commit themselves to any "ism" that offers selective salvation and a single path to life eternal. The majority of them have opted for universalism and a spirituality that belongs to everyone.

Today there are groups of metaphysicians and men and women hoping to retribalize in traditional Amerindian style in nearly every community in North America. The majority of them are interested only in concentrating on self-awareness and in promoting the true brotherhood. An entire generation has structured a new and vital reality for themselves. They will be prepared for the coming period of transition.

In his book *Uni-Chotometrics*, Eugene A. Albright describes his vision of the impending change, the Tomorrow which has been variously described and named throughout history as the New Age, the Advent of the New Man, the Millennium, the Great Purification.

Albright writes, "The next ... evolving technique of the human organism, will be the opening up of two specific functions which, up to this stage of development, have been latent.

"One of these is the capacity to control the environment completely; to cause matter in the environment to disintegrate and restructuralize directly on an energy level. The other is to structure the function of the body and replenish it without necessity for food, either plant or animal life."

Albright express his opinion that in the past there have been periods in which the vibratory rate was stepped up. "Many who cannot adjust to higher rated of vibration are destroyed," he says. "This may appear to be cruel, but nature and that which is natural, has always prevailed and it will prevail."

In my book, *Revelation: The Divine Fire,* I deal with contemporary prophets and revelators, men and women such as the Medicine people, who claim communication with Higher Intelligence. In my opinion, throughout history and in all lands, the revelatory experience has been designed to inform mankind of certain universal precepts.

1. There is a Higher Intelligence, or Energy Source, from which every man might draw power and inspiration.

2. Man has within him all that is necessary to establish harmony with Higher Intelligence, provided certain spiritual conditions are encouraged and maintained.

3. Man is one with all other men in spirit and has a sense of unity with all things. Man's soul is both universal and individual.

4. Man is evolving toward a New Age, that is, a dramatic progression in his evolution as a spiritual being. We are moving toward a state of mystical consciousness wherein every man shall be a god under God.

It is my belief that the central purpose of the revelatory process throughout history has been to lead *Homo sapiens* to the understanding that he can be so much more than a creature of conditioned reflexes, biochemical compounds, and glandular responses and that he is evolving as a spiritual being and progressing out of his old, physical limitations into a higher consciousness that is his by right of his cosmic inheritance.

The greatest lesson that the Medicine people—together with all the inspired men and women of history—have shared from their perspective of heightened consciousness has been that material, consensual reality is subject to dramatic change by the essential self of each individual. Each man and woman has the latent ability to shape a reality separate from that of the ordinary and the commonly accepted.

When one has absorbed this basic lesson and discovered his own techniques for application, his own Medicine, he has truly learned how to survive the coming time of Great Purification and how to hasten his own spiritual evolution.

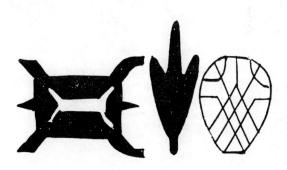

Many American Indians believe UFOs play a vital part in the prophecies of
their people and in the coming Earth changes. For centuries UFOs have been
seen over and around Indian reservations, and are taken for granted by the
spiritually minded such as Tahahlita who took this picture in September,
1972 over Grants Pass, Oregon.

CHAPTER EIGHTEEN

Transform Your Life Through Indian Magic

I have always been a great admirer of the works of Ralph Waldo Emerson. I think that he is perhaps the first of the truly American philosophers, yet he brought so many Eastern elements into the American mainstream. He took much of European and Asiatic thought and combined them into something rather distinctly American—or what has come to be know as American.

I think it is worth noting that Emerson, either consciously or unconsciously, seemed to present a kind of magical system that really worked. I believe Emerson was indeed a true magician in his vision of the Oversoul, wherein he sees this entity as not only an objective, cosmic energy, but also as being at the very interior of each individual—the Soul of the whole within humankind. Emerson saw then as every practitioner of magic must, the fundamental wholeness of the universe—the wholeness that dignifies and makes precious every fragment which participates in the whole.

There is definitely much of the microcosm and the macrocosm in the writings of Emerson. The very fact that we can exalt the lesser and the greater seems to be one of the key ideas that he repeats frequently. As the basis of his magic, he indicates that we must develop a certain form of concentration. We must learn to enter into the nature, the very identity, of the smallest particular, whereby we also presuppose the great expansion of the universe.

Emerson never suggested that we should lose ourselves in a great sea of details that would only make us more confused than we were when we began our quest. But he assumed that the greater consciousness will be able to bring to us a vision of it identity with the great unity, the great Oneness of the universe.

Emerson was the ideal of the Spiritual Seeker in that he insisted that everything must be practical, every bit of magical energy must be utilitarian. It must be workable. It must be something that can be applied.

There is also this thought in the magical system of the American Indians. The Indian way of life was both of necessity, and by choice, closely attuned to the environment in which the individual tribes lived. In order to establish and maintain their bond with the Earth Mother, the Indians were careful to establish contact with the spiritual forces of the land. They realized that to eat the produce of Earth or the creatures of Earth was to create a very real link-up with the Earth Mother herself. The spiritual beings which are associated with each environmental region were therefore brought into this oneness by a custom that was established in many North American tribes, that of offering the first fruits to either the various animal and vegetable spirits electively, or to the great spirit, the Manitou, the Wakan.

One of the most essential elements in Emerson's philosophical-magical system is his dual view of human experience. Emerson remarks that to lose oneself in any phenomenon, in any happening that is contemplated, only becomes creative if a high part of the psyche is able to maintain a contact with the universe which contains that phenomenon. Experience is meaningful, fertile, only when we hold to that which experiences. This principle Emerson applies on all levels of human life.

In any magical system, to immerse oneself totally in an experience is not power, but loss of power. This is part of the reason why a doctor must not treat his own wife or child ... why those whose healing powers originate from a more mystical or magical level often find that they are unable to heal those closest to them—or even themselves. And why a psychic sensitive is unable to read successfully and objectively for himself or herself.

I have heard so many aspiring metaphysicians who are misguided in this aspect. I have heard them say how they totally became *one* with the experience ... how they totally became one in empathy with another.

There are times when such a oneness is important. There are times when such a oneness can be truly beautiful and give an extra dimension and insight to your future apprehension of the universe or of an individual going through a particular kind of experience. But in order to have true power, the creative spiritual magician must always reserve a part of himself that is *detached*, that is *observing*, that is *listening* and *watching*, whatever the event in which he or she is involved. ***That is where the power lies!***

If you became immersed totally in an experience, you cannot judge it; you cannot deal with it. You may be swept up by the emotion. You may be overcome by the various elements of emotionality, of passion, that may be involved, that may be integral to the full sweep of that experience.

The spiritual magician does participate. He is more than an observer of actions around him. But in order to have full power, he must be *both* observer and participant at the same time.

As a practitioner of Indian magic, you must learn to develop a third ear as well as the third eye. You must be able to hear what you are saying as you say it. And you must be able to hear it from the perspective of those who listen to you. You must be able to see yourself as you conduct various activities. You must be able to comprehend and to relate to yourself as others see you, as others comprehend you and apprehend you.

All these things combine to give you power, but you lose the power if you become totally wrapped up in the emotion of events. You must present your magic in a detached, emotionless way.

I am not advocating that the spiritual magician becomes a machine, a computer, a cold, calculating, totally objective, rational being all of the time. There are times to become at one with an experience and to become at one with others. But when you are conducting Magic, when you are becoming a Medicine person and truly seek to transmutate energy, then you must remain detached. You must remain apart from the total flow of a happening or an occurrence if you truly seek to transmutate it.

If you are involved in circumstances that are so compelling that you are drawn almost like a magnet to give your complete intellectual and emotional involvement to them, then it may still be possible to free your magical awareness by going outside of your conscious personality.

Many scholars of the American Indian have noted that it was the custom of various tribes in times of general distress to appoint a special meeting, often at a sacred spot, where, after suitable songs and ritual acts had been performed, all would to to sleep for the night. Before entering into slumber they would direct their minds to the problem that was besetting them. In the morning, they would tell one another their dreams, and they would seek to assess them. Then by coming together and comparing the interpretations, they would arrive at a solution to their problem. The fact that the decision thus arrived at was felt to be the true solution was indicated by a marked change of spirit and attitude in those who were seeking the answers. Those who had arrived oppressed with anxiety, grief, or resentment would depart laughing and light-hearted—even though the night's revelation in the dream vision may well have confirmed the knowledge that dangers and difficulties were still to be endured.

The Indian in North America seems to have a particularly close sense of union with the universe, its great dimensions, the invisible powers, the solar and lunar forces, the star gods, the four cardinal points or directions. The practitioner of Indian magic in North America feels a strong link between the human and non-human occupants of the material world—animals, birds, trees, plants, winds and waters, rocks, earth, and fire. We see in Longfellow's *Hiawatha* many elements that are also found in the mythologies of the old world. There is Nakomis, daughter of the Moon, who has her place in the story, first as a bride then as mother, then as grandmother. There is the customary fight with the dragon or monster, represented by the combat with the great fish. There is the maize hero, Mondimin, who certainly is no stranger to those of us who know the myths of the great heroes.

Although the Medicine person in North America feels a great connection, a great harmony which amounts to a brotherhood, a sisterhood, an identification with various animals and plants in the region, the modern American, tragically, seems to become a more destructive creature. He looks at the trees and the streams and the animals on this continent and seems to assert his right to use them, to exploit the, to kill them; to clear the land, to burn the forest, to drive out the animals that exist there all in the name of progress. The spiritual magician, of course, is always one who can see father, one who has a view of the future, one who always looks at the big picture rather than the small picture, one who recognizes that all living creatures have a equal right to a place on this Earth.

Of course, it is not only animals that are in question when modern man begins to exercise the "rights" which are so destructive. It is not only the great redwood forest which are destroyed for stylish garden furniture or for fences around homes. Magnificent trees that have grown for centuries, towering trees that have stood on guard like wise guardians and sentinals, are chopped up for the faddish whims of men and women who wish to surround their homes with redwood fences.

The very fabric, the very matrix of our continent, the very web of existence, is being threatened by people who are thinking selfishly. Selfish thought is always destructive thought, not only to the individuals who feel the selfish sting and poison, but to the individual who sends out the venom—who first must endanger his own spirit with the acid of greed and selfishness.

Emerson, the great Spiritual Alchemist, believed that the purpose of philosophy (the purpose of magic as we would say, because it is all one) functions through the faculties of feeling and intellect—and finally through intuition itself—at a moment when there is a contact with the underlying essence of the marvelous energy that is all around us.

Here are two versions of an exercise that you might use the next time you are walking in the woods, the next time you are walking the desert, the next time you are standing by the ocean.

192

These exercises will help to get you in greater balance wit the Earth Mother and in greater harmony with the energies of nature.

Take a deep breath, just a comfortably deep breath, hold it for the count of three, then release it. Repeat this three times.

Begin to look North; look toward the North. Let your eyes go to the far, far horizon of the North. Begin to feel yourself growing as you look toward the North.

Visualize yourself stretching upward, as if you are, perhaps, a tall redwood tree. Stretch your arms out in front of you as if they are limbs stretching forth.

Imagine that you can touch the far horizon of the North. Then turning slowly, imagine that your arms stretch out and touch the horizon, the great pole of the horizon, as if you can brush the very farthest reaches of the horizon with your fingertips, as you move slowly around. Perhaps you are touching a forest, perhaps you are touching a cloud, perhaps you are touching the ocean. Perhaps you are touching the waters of a lake. Perhaps you are touching grasses on a rolling plane.

Wherever you touch, as you move slowly with your great arms stretching from horizon to horizon, let the Earth Mother know that you are aware of her. Bless her and all that you touch. Feel the energy moving out from you, blessing all that you touch. Feel the blessing returning to you.

Keep your eyes open as you move counter clockwise. Moving counter clockwise, feel your fingertips brush the farthest reaches that you can see with your eyes. As far as you can see with your eyes, touch with your fingertips.

Now close your eyes. Close your eyes and know that you are are a focal point. There is the great Earth Mother all around you. There is the great Sky Father above you, and all around you are energies seen and unseen, felt and only guessed at.

You, through your mind, constitute the focal point that touches the universe, that caresses the Earth Mother. Open all of your senses to receive the blessing that the Earth Mother sends back to you. Feel and know yourself to be the center of a great benevolent energy, which is consecrated by all that surrounds you.

At another time, wherever you are, wherever you are standing in nature, in the great out-of-doors, see yourself as if you are a pebble tossed into a great pool. Allow your consciousness to become the ripples that spread across the surface of this great pool. Your consciousness moves from the center of the pool to the farthest horizon, until you have formed a great circle. You are in the center, spreading forth with the great ripples of consciousness.

You are in the center, but now, like a great circular pool, you have touched all of the horizons, East, West, North, and South. You feel the circle of your awareness growing larger and larger. Larger and larger, until it touches as far as you can see. It touches all around you, horizon to horizon. You are aware of yourself only as a focal point to the midst of the great pool of time, the great pool of energy. Open your heart to the blessings that will return in the ripples that come from each horizon. Let the Earth Mother send back into the pool of energy, into the pool of greater consciousness, blessing after blessing, which will be like ripple after ripple returning to the center of your awareness.

As a practitioner of Indian magic, you will discover that the more aware you become, the more you will fell yourself to be a part of something bigger than all of humankind amassed. You will find yourself reaching beyond your body and turning in on an intelligence that appears to fill all of space.

You will find that communication can take place with a total disregard for distance. Perhaps this intelligence in space senses our needs; and from time to time, marvelous coincidences take place. Or our prayers are answered. Or everything just seems to work out by itself.

The cosmos operates according to divine principles, whether we know, understand, accept them or not. However, if you as a spiritual magician become conscious of being part of an Intelligence filling space, you can tap that energy and harness it with a greater degree of success. You can actually be less separated and more a part of this Intelligence. Simultaneously, your body will become less subject to the stresses that you impose upon it. With your consciousness, separateness, and more than natural mechanisms that less conscious creatures enjoy, you will be able to stand in your own light on Earth, and you will wonder why others around you who are less aware are complaining because it is dark.

How can you become more conscious of your identification with the Intelligence that fills space?

When you sit in quiet meditation, you are, in fact, attuning yourself to this Intelligence. Every time you spend a few minutes in quiet attunement with the cosmos, you are helping to undo the restricting attitude of

194

separateness, and you are permitting nature to flow more easily through you.

A good exercise to repeat on a daily basis to demonstrate your ability to join the seen and the unseen is to stand with your arms stretched forward, your palms down, then intone the universal sound *Ommmmmmm* in a long, drawn-out chant. *Ommmmmmm.*

Repeat this until you can actually feel tingling in the palms of your hands. Until the skin actually picks up auditory vibrations.

Then begin to project another type of energy toward your palms. Try to project a life force to your palms. Visualize the life force passing through your fingers, moving out to the palms of your hands. Focus on this until you begin to feel a tingling sensation—almost as if electrical vibrations are moving through you.

Next, begin to feel an actual palpable force moving out of your palms. Visualize a golden ball of energy, hovering just beyond the palms of your hands. Visualize this as a great energy of love. Then at this time in your exercise, at this stage of the experiment, begin to project this force to others.

Visualize that golden ball moving through the walls, through the ceiling, through space, and see it enveloping someone whom you are projecting (visualizing) in your mind. Visualize that golden globe of light surrounding that individual with love.

Perhaps you then can visualize an energy thread such as the Kahunas envision to symbolize the flowing out of Mana. See it flowing out from your body, flowing out from your energy source, flowing out from the palms of your hands, and then touching someone with connective energy.

This is a way to establish a telepathic connection. This is a way to cause someone to begin to think favorably about you. This is a good way of causing someone in whom you may have a romantic interest to feel your love.

Visualize white threads moving out from the palms of your hands, or if you wish from your solar plexus. See these white threads moving through space, touching, connecting you with the loved one—connecting you with someone with whom you wish telepathic contact. Visualize the white threads moving and touching that individual, forming a network, forming an actual telephone line between you and that individual.

As a positive magician, of course, you will know only of the power of good. You will not recognize any power of evil. When you are a practitioner of Indian magic, recognizing only the good around you and only the good that you will do, then your entire mind, body, spirit, triad will be more receptive to cosmic illumination.

Physicists continue to probe the nature of light. What is light really?

Spiritual teachers have long been able to harness light's energies in a metaphysical way. Jesus, Mohammed, St. Paul, numerous spiritual heroes experienced light in tremendous intensity.

Walt Whitman was surely one who saw the light in its fullest cosmic expression.

In my book *Revelation: The Divine Fire,* I speak of the phenomenon of the divine light that can move over one and bring all illumination.

As a simple exercise to help bring about illumination and the manifestation of the light in your life, relax very deeply in the privacy of your room. Conduct a two-minute meditation in which you visualize a brilliant light surrounding your head, surrounding your body.

Visualize that light moving around you. You know it is the light from the very heart of the universe. You know that it is the light of goodness. It is the light of unconditional love.

Visualize that light moving into you. Visualize that light actually becoming a part of you. Visualize yourself becoming at one with the light.

One of the most important disciplines and learnings of the Indian magic person is to learn to break the shackles of time by escaping linear time and to move into the nonlinear sense of time. After one moves into the spiral time sense, it becomes easier to transcend the "I," to move away from ego and become at one with the very cosmic pulse of the universe.

To become a spiritual magician is to give service to all of life. Recognize that there really is no such thing as work. Recognize that there really is no such thing as work. It is a privilege for you to celebrate life in an active manner. Rejoice that you are allowed to serve life, for you are serving your *own* life and for your *own* true freedom. When you work in service for all of humankind, you are perpetually given the opportunities to balance what you have not done in the past, but should have done. You are also given opportunities to correct what you have done incorrectly. The spiritual magician has a three-fold service to the source of All-That-Is, to the world of humanity, and to himself or herself.

Everything that the Medicine person does must have an application to the greater universe about him. He must exist at once in the microcosm and in the macrocosm. To have a practical application for all action is the basic understanding of one of the divine laws which brings knowledge and illumination to individuals.

It is such an understanding of the law of application that will enable you to begin to develop true self-mastery.

The divine laws do not simply apply themselves to you. You must begin to serve as a conduit with which to focus the divine energies in order to get results. And, as every spiritual magician knows, just wishing does not make it so.

Whatever task you set out to fulfill in life, it is vital that you first call forth protection against wrong, vibratory action. Negative vibrations are all about us in the very atmosphere—especially in large cities where there is so much chaotic thinking, so much violence, so much stress and tension.

Mastery is only gained through conscious effort. You must take a certain application and hold to it, so as never to lose your centralized focus of power. It is not possible to transform from one to another what your own application has released, any more than you can eat for anyone else.

Long ago the great masses of humankind turned away from the light. The very divine laws demand that an effort be made on their part to again return to the source of All-That-Is and to attain eternal freedom.

Prayers are usually supplication to an omnipotent God. You must come to establishes a firm connection to the source of All-That-Is so that you may command the powers of light into action.

There is a big difference in the manifestation of power between simply making a supplication and asking a diety to fulfill a request, then moving with confidence and power to command the light into fulfilling that which is needed. Ask only for that which is for your good and your gaining. You will have to make your maximum effort, and then assistance can be given from energies higher than your own.

It is your doing that brings forth the light. Desire is God in action. But desire blended with human quality becomes human desire. Always give your greatest love and your greatest effort toward the source of All-That-Is.

When you put the Source first and foremost in all of your activities, then the things that you truly need for your good and your gaining will always be at hand.

Your attunement to the Source is the key that releases the divine fire. Pour forth love to the Source. That is the golden key that will open every door to every secret treasure that you desire.

Try always to bring the greater consciousness of the Source into everything that you do and acknowledge the Source while you are doing it.

Give conscious recognition to the Source, doing everything through you.

Three times a day you should practice feeling the presence of the Source moving through you.

Remember always that it is through continued practice of negativity that humankind has created its limitations and distresses. Disease, disasters, imperfections in the world are the results of energy that has been limited. The Spiritual Alchemist commands the energies that he senses about him and focuses light energy so that he may change and become perfect.

When you have called the higher energies of the Source into action, be alert for any promptings, any feelings that you may have that will direct special activities, special action, on your part. Then, once you have sensed such promptings, fulfill that action.

Learn to understand and to recognize that every impulse that you receive is not always from the Source. If it becomes stronger as you give attention to it, then likely it is. But if the energy of it begins to ebb and to fade, then quite likely it is not.

When your true inner being prompts you that a thing is wrong, stand by that warning, regardless of who may speak out against you. Premonitions may be a prompting from your higher self or from a higher intelligence contacting you through more profound levels of your consciousness.

When you have a premonition, just remember that it does not mean that it *must* take place. It may only be a warning or a prompting that brings a particular matter to your attention so that you can apply the various laws and transmute it, thereby avoiding any unfavorable action which you may have foreseen.

When you seek to command the energies, remember that to do so requires more than a simple saying of words. You must feel what you are saying. You must *feel* the energy as you direct it into definite thought forms, which someday will be translated into reality.

You must be wary that you do not get into a state of consciousness in which you simply command the higher energies for the sake of release. You must never command the energies unless you have a true and rightful purpose in doing son.

When you command the energies, remember that you must always follow through when the energy is released. If the energy should ever be released from you without enough unconditional love, then it would be best to call back that energy until you have blessed it and sent it forward once again.

If you send for the energies simple to make a good appearance, a good impression upon someone else, it is quite probable that you will have unfavorable results.

The results will be improper and unrealized because you have placed your attention on the wrong type of motivating impulse.

Give your higher self the reins, instead of your trying to make all the directions yourself. Let the little Genie within you become your captain. When you become tense, you will rely upon nervous energy to drive forth the power and the light.

Remember always to remain humble. Constantly remind your ego that it is the Source action through you that is the great practitioner. Humbleness, of course, does not mean that you must compromise with evil or with improper human conditions. But humility before the Source of All-That-Is will give you the proper attitude by which to be a more fully functioning and complete practitioner of Indian magic.

Never seek to justify your mistakes or anything that you have performed incorrectly. Never be said to be unjust, even by your enemies. Never defend a thought, word, or deed of another that you believe to be wrong.

How shall you judge a thought, word, or deed? If it creates disharmony in you, in others, or in the perpetrator of the act, it is wrong.

Be fearless, knowing that the Source of All-That-Is sends its light to work through you. When you know that this mighty power can operate through your human agency, then you know that nothing negative can stand against you. You can be firm and determined, and you can compel all that is inharmonious about you to become harmonious.

Call forth the energy of the divine Source of All-That-Is to manifest in every detail of your daily life.

When you, as a true magician seek to give commands in the name of the light, you should do it in a firm and positive manner, but not with an exertion of human will. When you use the human aspect of yourself in directing the light, you give a qualification to the stream of light from the source of All-That-Is, that is being moved through you.

You must keep your channel pure. And you must understand that the Source of All-That-Is must not be distracted by ego, or by your desire to create a particular kind of appearance to please or to influence another.

It is in the silence of meditation that the most energy is concentrated. When you enter the great silence, feel and know that you are surrounded by the divine fire from the Great Spirit, the Source of All-That-Is. Know that you are becoming more a part of the central sun of the cosmic universe. It is in the silence that you find the power of light and the balance and the love of the Earth Mother.

Feel the silence all through you, focused in the very center of your being, the very pivotal point of your spirit. Be still and know that the Source of All-That-Is exists strongest in the silence.

To enter the silence, your emotional body has to be stilled as well as all mental activity. Learn to feel and to be at one with the Source of All-That-Is.

Turn your attention to the flame in your heart, and then, in consciousness, ascend a ray of purple light to the Source of All-That-Is. Feel closeness with it. Then feel the points of light in every cell in your body become connected with the points of light in your Higher Self. See your own Higher Self connected, as if by a thread of light, to the Great Spirit, the Source of All-That-Is. And as you contemplate this, feel a great sense of oneness, of closeness, of attunement with higher intelligence. This is the essence of Indian magic.

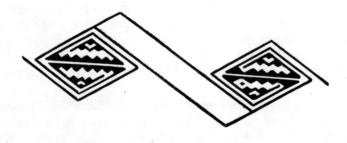